The **Guardian**
BOOK OF PUZZLES

The **Guardian**

BOOK OF PUZZLES

Christopher Maslanka
illustrated by Ian Anderson

Fourth Estate · London

For Jerzy and Jadwiga Zieniuk

First published in Great Britain in 1990 by
Fourth Estate Limited
289 Westbourne Grove
London W11 2QA

The Guardian Book of Puzzles
1. Quiz games
I. Maslanka, Christopher
793.73

ISBN 1-872180-72-8

Typeset in Erhardt by York House Typographic,
Hanwell, London W7
Printed and bound by Clays Ltd, Bungay, Suffolk

Contents

I extend my thanks to all the faithful readers of my *Pyrgic Puzzles* column in *The Guardian* and *New Scientist*, especially to the young readers of *The Early Times*, for their many letters of appreciation, encouragement and criticism and to all others who wrote in correcting my many Homeric nods, real or imagined.

My thanks also to David Freeman of BBC Radio Oxford and the many listeners to our weekly phone-in puzzle programme on Friday afternoons; and to my checkers, Pete Bevin and Sharon Curtis who have, I hope, saved me from the careless mistakes which normally follow my use of the words 'of course' in any proof. Lastly I thank Ione Noble for all her help in the preparation of this manuscript.

Chapter One

As the sun rose up from behind Pembish Hall, it raised several
questions. Here are a few of them . . .

1   Professor Pembish, inventor and eccentric, was born in the middle of March and has a birthday only once every four years.

Explain this. **H**

2   'That's nothing,' said Punnish, his retainer, 'my grandfather was eight years old on his first birthday.'

How can one account for *that*? **H**

3   Would it be possible for one's grandfather to be younger than one's father?

4   Whilst we are on the topic of age, if a man was 30 the day before yesterday and will be 33 next year what day is it and when is his birthday? **H**

5   A says to his brother B:

'You were born only minutes after me, of the same parents on the same day of the month of the same year in the same place. We have no brothers and we are not twins.'

Explain this.

6   'I have as many brothers as sisters,' says A to his sister B.

'That's nothing,' replies his sister, who always has to be one up, 'I have twice as many brothers as sisters.'

How many brothers and sisters are there? **H**

7   Mrs Weeks has seven children whom she has named in the order of their birth:

Monday, Tuesday, Wednesday, Thursday, Friday, Saturday and Sunday.

On multiplying together all their ages in years (whole numbers only, please) one obtains the number 6591.

Given that today is the birthday of all seven, how many of the children are triplets? **H**

8   'Now if today were *my* birthday,' thought Pembish as he dressed in front of the mirror, 'I'd want it to last *all day*. In fact, I'd want it to last as long as possible. However, as there are only 24 hours in a day I suppose that limits one's birthday to 24 hours, too.'

However, it dawned on him, much more slowly than the speed of light, that one's birthday could, in principle, be stretched out quite a bit longer than this.

How long could one's birthday be made to last, given that the day remains 24 hours long? **H**

*Astronomer Seymour Stars likes to phrase this question in a more mischievous way: How long does a day last on Earth?

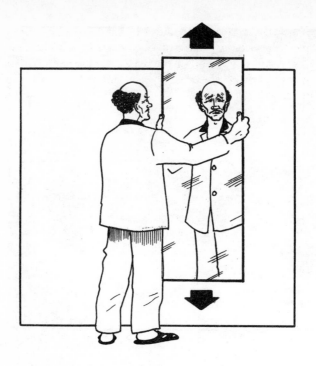

9   Pembish's wall mirror is quite* flat and the image is undistorted. When he stands in front of it, he can just see himself in it from top to toe. Given that he is 6 foot tall, how long is the mirror?

How high up the wall** must the mirror be fixed? **H**

*'quite flat' meaning 'perfectly flat' rather than 'flattish'.

**The wall is quite vertical, of course, and the floor horizontal. You may assume, too, that Pembish stands up vertically, rather than at an angle.

10 'I must say,' said Pembish, 'I feel a great deal younger than I am. A bit like dear old Uncle Percy, really. *His* birthdays were out of step right from the outset. Twelve months after he was born he had already been one year old for two months.'

Explain this. **H**

11 Pembish draws a figure 8 on a piece of paper. Under his (powerful) magnifying glass it looks twice as big. He then draws another figure on the piece of paper and looks at it through the magnifying glass. But it looks no bigger than before. What had he drawn?

12 As he is finishing dressing, Pembish hears the postman coming up the drive. On his dressing table is an airmail letter which he wants posting, so he calls to him from the open window.

'Just drop it, Mr Pembish,' the postman yells back up to him.

Pembish leans out of the window and finds himself directly above the postman.

How ought Pembish release the letter? As in (A) or as in (B)? **H**

13   Among the letters that morning was one from Pembish's
      Aunt Agatha threatening a visit. 'I suppose we'd better hang
      her portrait – you know, the one she gave us for Christmas,'
      said Pembish to Punnish, who had just come in from the
      garden and was leaving a trail of dirty bootprints across the
      kitchen floor.

      'I can make a frame if you want,' rejoindered Punnish. 'I
      seem to remember that each side was an exact whole
      number of inches and the perimeter in inches was equal to
      the area in square inches.' 'Yes, and it's rectangular not
      square, more's the pity,' burbled Pembish.

      What are the dimensions of the frame Punnish will have to
      make? **H**

14   Pembish decided to have a boiled egg and some toast for breakfast. *Unfortunately*, he had mislaid his watch.* *Fortunately*, there were two egg-timers in the kitchen, one marked '4 minutes' and the other marked '7 minutes'. *Unfortunately*, he liked his eggs to be boiled for exactly 5 minutes. *Fortunately*, he knew how to time exactly 5 minutes using the two timers in combination. In fact Pembish not only timed his egg to perfection but also adopted the strategy taking least time. Can you say how he achieved this and how long it took? **H**

*Not as bad as mislaying the egg.

15   When Pembish went to the refrigerator he remembered
     that Punnish had boiled some eggs the day before for a
     picnic which had subsequently had to be called off because
     of rain. Well, the boiled eggs had been put back in the fridge
     with the unboiled ones, hadn't they? Being an orderly type
     and not wishing to reboil an egg by mistake, he decided to
     sort the eggs into hard-boiled and unboiled.

Luckily he knew a way of going about this without breaking
any.

How? **H**

*Punnish japishly remarked that it was odd how eggs could be
unboiled although you couldn't unboil them. Pembish's reply was
to send him out into the garden.

13

16   Pembish needed a few minutes to collect his thoughts, so he sent Punnish out into the garden with four seedlings to plant.

'How do you want them planted?' asked Punnish as Pembish locked him out.

'Oh, in such a way that each and every one of them is equidistant from each of the other three!' retorted Pembish through the letter-box.

However, five minutes later, there it was, a tap on the window: Punnish had returned, mission accomplished.

How had he fulfilled Pembish's conditions? **H**

17 The odometer on Pembish's old car shows hundreds, tens and units. When he bought it, it read 000. After completing 1,000 miles it read 000 again. As he and Punnish encarred that morning, Punnish couldn't help noticing that the odometer read 686. 'That is a palindromic* number,' he remarked to Pembish as they reversed out of the garage. 'It reads the same if you reverse the order of the digits. I wonder whether that happens very often?'

Pembish was so distracted by this question that he drove all the way down the long drive in reverse.

How many different readings between 000 and 999 (both included) read the same backwards as forwards?

*According to Szklowski, 'palindromic' comes from the Greek words *palin* = *back again* and *dromos* = *road* or *way*. Numbers which read the same when the digits are read in reverse order are palindromic numbers, or palindromes. There can be verbal palindromes, too. (See Puzzle No. 87).

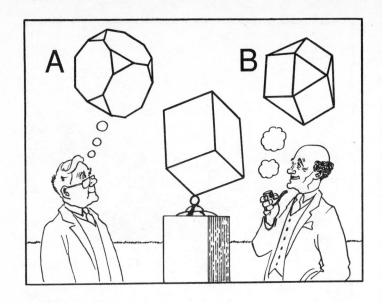

18   Originally each of Pembish's gateposts had a cube on top.
      'Admittedly a cube *is* a little dull,' remarked Pembish.
      Punnish suggested they cut off the corners of the cube, so
      producing another symmetrical figure. 'Yes,' answered
      Pembish, 'each cube would then have fourteen faces. That
      would make them *tessaracaidecahedra*. I must say, I like the
      sound of that. You see, *Tessaracaideca* is not only Greek for
      fourteen but it also has fourteen letters in it. That seems
      very appropriate. However, there are two ways of cutting off
      the corners. We can cut off a little (A) or we can cut off a lot
      (B).'

      (Punnish didn't hear any of this as he was already running
      to fetch a saw.)

      How many edges and corners do each of the proposed new
      gateposts have (a) if Pembish decides on plan A, and (b) if
      he decides on plan B? **H**

19 Can you *construct* a single-word anagram of CUTTING CORNERS?

20 A CUBOID has six faces just as its name has six letters. Can you think of another three-dimensional figure having as many faces as its name has letters? **H**

Chapter Two

As Pembish and Punnish drove along, Pembish couldn't help wondering what the other inhabitants of Camford were up to that bright and sunny morning . . .

21   John Bayleaf as his wont ever will be, was about to don a pair
      of odd socks. Not that there was anything odd about each
      sock, *taken separately*; but that's just what they were: taken
      separately from a bedside drawer in which they lived side by
      side, black socks and white socks only, in commingled but
      contented chaos. This morning he is down to his last four
      socks and the chances of picking at random a pair of white
      socks are $\frac{1}{2}$. What are the chances of his choosing, instead, a
      pair of black socks? **H**

22   Telephonopoulos came across some telephone cable in the quad of St Gaderine's. 'There's at least half a drum of good cable there, all wound onto the spool neatly and uniformly, just like cotton on a bobbin.'

This remark, addressed to himself, set him thinking. You see, if the drum were on a fixed axle permitting the drum to *turn* only, pulling the free end of the cable would cause the cable to unwind from the drum, which would turn anti-clockwise as viewed by the reader. But the drum, reasoned Telephonopoulos, is *not* on a fixed axle; indeed it is standing on the revered and horizontal paving stones of the St Gaderine's quad.

If Telephonopoulos pulls on the free end of the cable with a firm pull but not so strongly that the drum slips, what will happen? Will the cable unwind from the drum? And which way will the drum roll: to the left or to the right? Or will it stand still unless pulled so firmly that it slips across the ground?

23   The postman found himself with a puzzling parcel. Instead of an address it bore the inscription:

'To the only house in Mauritius Crescent the sum of the digits of whose number is exactly twice their product. By 'product' I mean, of course, the number obtained by multiplying the digits together.'

To the postman's surprise he found himself delivering it to his own house.

At which number did the postman live and what was the greatest number of houses there could have been in the Crescent?* **H**

*The house numbers in Mauritius Crescent start at 1 and continue with 2, 3, 4 and so on up to the highest house number. Every house has a whole number only as its number and there are no numbers (or houses) missing.

24   Helen Highwater's car wouldn't start and she was standing in a bus queue on her way to St. Awayday's School for the Upwardly Mobile. She noted that if the man at the front with the big ears were to go to the back there would be twice as many people behind as in front, and if instead the woman at the back were to go to the front there would be twice as many queuers in front as behind.

What position did she have in the queue?

25 'Neither too far to the left nor too far to the right,' intoned Mr Triode as he walked across Camford Town Square towards the august offices of the *Camford Journal*. As if to illustrate this very dictum, he crossed the square in a straight line which divided the paved area into exact halves.

At what point did he begin his walk? **H**

26 'That's curious,' commented Tunku Varadarajan, who accounted himself quite rightly a connoisseur of cricket, 'that headline is ambiguous. Either they are claiming that Thambo has scored 100 runs and the "!" signifies unjustified surprise, or else they claim that he has scored 100! runs, which, even in his case, would be such an amazing achievement that it would merit several extra exclamation marks!'*

If Thambo had really scored 100! runs, and the *Daily Grind* had written out this number of runs in full, how many zeroes would have appeared at the end of the number? **H**

*In mathematics *N*! (pronounced '*N* factorial' or '*N* bang') stands for $1 \times 2 \times 3 \times 4$ and so on up to *N*, so that, for example, $3! = 1 \times 2 \times 3 = 6$; $5! = 1 \times 2 \times 3 \times 4 \times 5 = 120$ and $11! = 1 \times 2 \times 3 \times 4 \times 5 \times 6 \times 7 \times 8 \times 9 \times 10 \times 11 = 39916800$.

27   A farmer was interviewing young Master Metal,* sent to
      him on a government employment scheme. 'I sees you has
      readin' and 'rithmetic,' ventured the farmer, 'so let's see
      you do this sum:

      **'All pigs is pigs, but some pigs is sows. I 'ave pigs in
      this 'ere sty. If you multiply the number of pig snouts
      by the number of pig trotters and then multiply by the
      number of sow's ears you gets 128.**

      'If you can tell me how many pigs I have there and how
      many is sows, you can start on cleanin' 'em out.'

      So Master Metal did and he did. How many pigs were there
      and how many of them were sows? **H**

      *Readers of *The Pyrgic Puzzler* will no doubt recognise this as the
      very same Master Metal who cut his father's 78 rpm recording of
      Horace Toccato neatly into halves with a saw. I am pleased to
      report that his job on the farm was a success and marked the
      beginnings of an eventual rehabilitation into polite society.

28   Mr Metal was on his way to Beale & Endalls to buy some
      second hand 78 rpm records for his old wind-up gramo-
      phone. 'I shall buy Chopin, Chopin and more Chopin,' he
      sighed blissfully. 'Then I must go and buy something else,
      now what was it?'

      When Mr Metal finally remembered what else he had to
      buy that morning he was amused to note that its name could
      be made by rearranging the letters of the phrase MORE
      CHOPIN into one word.

      What is the word?

29   'There's something very wrong with these four weights,' declared the post-mistress as Miss Bathpale entered the corner post-office at Dinge-Wittering.

'You can tell it straightway by trying to balance them against each other. Look, the 50gm weight balances exactly against these two, as it should. But when I try to balance the 45gm weight against *these* two, it goes down when it ought to balance!'*

Assuming one weight is at fault and no more, which is the culprit, and is it too heavy, or too light?

*The post-mistress uttered this last sentence with a sense of great outrage, which only goes to show how quiet and uneventful life normally is in this sleepy corner of the county.

30 Mr Buttermilk is so convinced that his poems will be plagiarised if left lying about that he uses all sorts of ingenious codes to conceal their artistic value from the casual observer. Even the titles of his poems have to be disguised so as not to give the game away. His usual trick with titles comprising two words consists in writing their letters down intermingled in such a way that if you cross out the letters belonging to one word it leaves the letters of the other in the right order.

He was just on the point of entrusting a poem to the post when he realised that he had not yet decoded the title. It had to catch the post to make the deadline, but the poem in question had been written so long ago that he couldn't remember what its title was:

DIMSTEAMORIENTS

Can you help?

31   The Schools Inspector was inspecting a display of the children's work in Miss Grammatica's class. Each picture had been painted during class time and had by it a neat label in block capitals stating what the picture was of.

He inspected cats, dogs, flowers and dinosaurs before finally arriving in front of one which was harder to interpret. The label wasn't exactly helpful, either:

At first he couldn't make head or tail of the picture or the label until one of the pupils pointed out what had happened.

What had happened? What was in the picture? **H**

32 Goody-Goody Major averages 80% on his first four examination papers and is determined to bump up his average to 85% with the fifth.

What mark must he get in his last paper?

33   In Whitewell's bookshop the assistant was setting out on a table copies of *The Benthic Axolotl* by William McCandy. The books were piled in such a way that if you stood on either side of the stacks spines and non-spines alternated. The assistant counted ten spines on one side of the stack and then, absent-mindedly, went around the table and counted ten non-spines.

How many books *must* there have been in the stack?

34   Colonel Plantpott-Smythe was daydreaming by his hock
and seltzer when he overheard the following:

'Oh, he has two lovely daughters now. And do you know,
their first names are anagrams of each other. Cornelia, the
one that you spoke to earlier on the telephone, is the elder.'

Plantpott couldn't help wondering what the name of the
younger one was.

What was it?

35 'That means our fathers are our husbands and our fathers are the fathers of our children.' Father O'Bubblegumm almost fell from the pulpit when he overheard this remark. Luckily the organist was on hand to explain with a diagram how these things had come to pass and he soon saw that nothing untoward had happened in the parish.

Can you explain the remark?

36   Mr Mayhem, proprietor of the Café Olé, was examining the
wholesaler's bill very carefully over his morning mocha. It
was for a whole number of pounds, a number consisting of
four odd digits. But that was not the only thing odd about it.

'But it's for exactly nine times too much!' he exclaimed.

The wholesaler peered closely at it. 'No harm done,' he
replied jauntily. 'If I cross the first digit off the total, it will
be correct.'

So he did, and to Mr Mayhem's amusement, it was, and so
he paid it.

How much did he pay? **H**

37 Mr Striker has managed to give up smoking. As a form of displacement activity, he now does match puzzles.

'Can you,' he asks a passer-by, 'make five equilateral triangles from nine matches?'

To his surprise, the stranger not only succeeds in doing this, but also goes on, as a tour de force, to make seven equilateral triangles with the same nine matches.

Can you show how *each* of these feats was performed? **H**

*As Szklowski points out, an equilateral triangle is one whose three sides are all of the same length.

38   Mr Zolyakar was thinking about a commission he had
      received to build a patio in the form of a stepped triangle out
      of slabs 1 metre square. The patio was to be flat and the
      slabs were not to overlap. The triangle was to be right-
      angled and only the longest side was to be stepped; the two
      shorter sides were to have straight edges. As if that were not
      enough, the perimeter in metres was to equal the number
      of square metres in the area.

      How many slabs would be required? **H**

39   'I wonder,' said Didipotamus to himself as he stood in front
of his whiteboard, scratching his head with a piece of chalk,
'what the largest proper fraction would be if it used all the
digits from 0 to 9 inclusive once and once only.'

He knew that a proper fraction was one in which the top
(numerator) was smaller than the bottom (denominator), as
with:

$$\frac{15098}{24376}$$

But that wasn't the answer to his question.

What was? **H**

40   The librarian at Camford library was being told by Miss Grammatica all about the Landors' new boy triplets.

Now the Landors had already had twin girls whom they had named Alice and Celia. They had named their second pair of twins Myra and Mary. Then came Amy and May and then Leon and Noel.

'And I think I know *just* what they will name their new boy triplets,' trilled Miss Grammatica in a nervous whisper.

Any suggestions? **H**

Chapter Three

Pembish and Punnish soon arrived at the market and set about their shopping . . .

41   Pembish was rather surprised to see the sign outside the
      fruiterer's:

         pineapple and mango : £2.00

         starfruit and pineapple: £1.60

         mango and starfruit: £1.20

      Assuming the prices were consistent, how much was each
      of the fruits? **H**

42   Meanwhile Mr Telephonopoulos was in the breakfast room of St Gaderine's, broaching a huge jar of his favourite Oakleaf honey. As usual he was talking about telephones.

'Have you noticed how in Camford all the old 5-digit telephone numbers began with a 4 but have now been converted to 6-digit numbers by the mere addition of an initial 2?' asked Telephonopoulos.

'Ooh yes,' twinkled Stars. 'I'm a down-to-earth sort of fellow and it suits me right down to the ground. You see, I'm always forgetting my telephone number. I don't ever ring myself up, after all. But now if I forget it, thanks to that initial 2 I now have a 6-digit number divisible by all the integers from 1 to 12 inclusive.'

'Oh,' said Telephonopoulos, 'so what is your number?'

Can you help Stars work it out? **H**

43   David Freeman was preparing to go on the air at Radio
Camford. He had a stack of 10 CDs in his hands and was
shuffling them. This is the way he was doing it:

He dealt the top disc onto the desk, without turning it over.
The next disc went to the bottom of the stack, without being
turned over. The next disc went, unturned, onto the desk to
the right of the one already there. And so on. When there
were no more discs in his hands, the row on the desk read,
from where he was sitting:

FBFBFBFBFB

(where 'F' stands for 'Front' and 'B' for 'Back').

What was their initial order?

44   Intrigued by the strange card in the window of Ann Teak's
      shop, the collector entered. In a dark corner of the shop he
      caught sight of an engraving, and as he peered to read the
      date on it he failed to realise at first that he was viewing it in
      a mirror. As a result, although he saw correctly that it was
      14th century, he thought that it was 27 years older than it
      was.

      What was the date (year) on the engraving? **H**

45 Kugelbaum came across a football lying on the pavement. 'Clearly,' he said to himself out loud, 'each and every pentagon is regular and of the same size as each and every other pentagon, and each and every hexagon is regular and the same size as each and every other hexagon. You can't count them very easily, but with a little common sense, if you are on the ball, you will be able to tell me how many hexagons there are altogether.'

How many hexagons are there on the surface of the ball? **H**

46 At the very moment Mrs Puttylump was returning from a race meeting. She had bet on three successive races, each time losing $\frac{2}{3}$ of the money she had. After the third race (No Regrets, 10-1) she was left with 50p. **H**

How much had she lost? **H**

47   Professor Yamamoto was winding up a lecture on *The Use of Intelligent Laziness in Mathematics*. He wrote up on the board the following multiplication as a challenge for his students:

81,624,324,048,566,472,808,896 × 12.5

Can you solve it in less than two minutes? **H**

48   Father O'Bubblegumm is at St Toad-in-the-Hole examining the design for a stained glass window which consists of a large circle and four small circles symmetrically placed within the larger as shown. The four smaller circles touch the outer circle and also meet at its centre.

The four 'petals' labelled Y are in yellow glass, the four parts labelled B are in blue and four parts labelled R are red.

'According to Mr Zolyakar,' mused the priest, 'there will be a total of 400 square centimetres of yellow glass in the window. It takes the eye of faith, but I think I see how much blue glass there will be, yet, then again, how can I be *sure*?'

What will the area of blue glass be? **H**

49   In the library of St Swott's, under a stuffed Coelacanth presented by mistake to that College by a myopic visiting dignitary, all on a shelf of their own, the ten volumes of the *Encyclopaedia Smartipantica* stand alone. Every day the volumes are to be found in a different order. 'If only,' sighed the librarian one day to the bursar, 'I had a hot dinner for every possible ordering of that encyclopaedia!'

How many hot dinners would that be? **H**

50   'I have no difficulty whatsoever remembering the combina-
      tion of my bicycle lock,' PC Klepto told himself as he undid
      the lock and walked off with it leaving his bicycle unpro-
      tected where it was, leaning against the wall of the Master's
      garden in St Gaderine's. 'All I have to remember is that it is
      a six-digit number consisting of a pair of 3s separated by
      three digits, a pair of 2s separated by two digits, and a pair of
      1s separated by one digit. Yes, yes, I know what you are
      going to say,' he told himself. 'There are two such numbers.
      Well, mine is the smaller of the two.'

      What is his number?

51 Dikmas Lanka, painter extraordinaire and genius in his own lunchtime, was redecorating Rabbi Yonkers' house. He needed six pints of light grey paint, which his customer had defined as two parts of white to one part black. Now sometimes Dikmas' left hand does not know what his right hand is doing, and today was just such an occasion. While his left hand was mixing in two pints of white his right hand was busy mixing in four pints of black.

'Oy,' said the Rabbi. 'A painter noch and such a bad mixer. I ask him mix me light grey and he mixes me dark grey. Nebechal! I want you mix me two parts white to one part black and not two parts black to one part white!' Now, on the one hand, Dikmas *could* throw the six pints of paint away and start all over again. On the other hand, he could add six pints of white to the mixture and then throw *half* of *that* away, again wasting six pints. But he did not want to look a complete balatron* in front of the Rabbi.

How can he proceed so as to waste as little paint as possible?
H

---

*a fool

52

52 Carmel Quantum was visiting the Rogues' Gallery to check
that her sculptures had been correctly set out for her
forthcoming exhibition. She was not pleased to see her
masterpiece *The Three Musketeers*, which, according to the
catalogue, consisted of '*four* black and white cubes'. At first
she thought that someone had made off with d'Artagnan.
Then she realised what had happened.

What *had* happened?

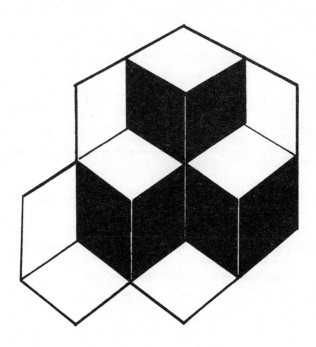

53 Mr Zolyakar glanced out of the window of his shed and saw the scene depicted above. He tried to deduce the number of slabs in the stack. The slabs, of identical dimensions, were stacked so that there were no gaps between them. The stack was 'a rectangular parallelepiped': every face was a rectangle with a right angle between two faces where they meet.

How many slabs were there?

54 St Awayday's has a magnetic blackboard. A missile launched by Genghis struck the board with such a thud that the digits and arithmetical signs all fell off. Of course, Noggie Norris* snitched, and a very patient Miss Highwater made Genghis pick them all up and stick them back on the board. So far he has not got very far with reconstructing the sum.

Can you help?

55 Unfortunately for young Genghis, no sooner had he sorted out the previous puzzle than Noggie Norris* pointed out that there had been a 6 on the board too and so Genghis had had to start again. Also, unfortunately, $5 \times 61 = 324$ was not quite right.

What should it be?

*Later to become Sir Ron Norris.

56   Padelyerownkanuski, 'The Punt Pole', hires out punts and
quants by the hour. The maximum punting speed is four
kilometres per hour in still water, and the river flows at a
leisurely two kilometres per hour.

If you hire a punt for four hours and you wish to spend
exactly two hours of that over a picnic with Amelia Earache,
what is the greatest distance from the boathouse that your
picnic could take place

(a) upstream?

(b) downstream?

Note for the Punter:

*It is just your luck that Ms Earache always insists that she be
punted at the maximum possible speed; besides, you would not
want to be a stick in the mud, would you? Second, you must
return the punt on time. As a misprint in Gertrood Phyllis-
Stein's romantic blockbuster,* Hooray for Henry! *says: 'Punc-
tuality is the thief of time.' Besides, to be late is to belate is to
belate. But I digress . . .*

57   The Reverend Eli Pet was wending his way across the Parks to St Gaderine's and to lunch when he came across a bench bearing the following inscription:

> ORE STABIT FORTIS ARARE PLACET
> ORE STAT

Now Eli had read all the Latin authors that that seat of learning could possibly offer. He had read Atticus Idioticus and Pincius Percius. He had translated the whole of the Rucksack Edition of the *Encylopaedia Smartipantica* into Latin and back again to see if it made any difference.* Why, he could practically order croissants and coffee in Latin. But the quotation, strange yet familiar, stumped him.

What does it mean?

*It didn't.

58 Tunku Varadarajan was by this time making his way across the Parks towards St Gaderine's when he came across a football 'perched atop a grassy knoll' as Mr Buttermilk would have put it in one of his *Odes to Objets Trouvés* (Garlic Press, £17.89). A fair depiction of the football is seen above.

As Tunku was not slow to realise, the ball consisted of pieces of leather, all the same size and shape, sewn together to form a rough sphere.

Three questions formed in his mind:

(a) How many pieces of leather did the football comprise (i.e. pieces of the form abcd)?

(b) At how many points on the ball's surface did one seam abut another (i.e. how many T-junctions are there like the one at b)?

(c) At how many points on the ball's surface did three seams meet (i.e. how many Y-junctions are there like the one at c)?

59 Mr Sharawaggi, the University Guide, was earnestly lecturing a crowd of tourists on the obvious merits of Jacob Arneson's design of St Gaderine's, one of the more modern colleges.

'Those bricks look non-standard,' a wag piped up facetiously. 'Do you know what their volume is?'

'I don't,' answered the Guide, disconcertedly consulting his battered copy of *Mein Campus.**

'Well, do you know the lengths of the sides then?' continued the heckler. 'If you tell us the lengths of the sides, we can work out the volume by multiplying them together.'

'I don't have a ruler,' replied the Guide testily, 'but I seem to remember the areas of the different faces are 110, 52.5 and 231 square centimetres.' So saying, he turned around to march off, but instead stepped straight into the moat.

What is the volume of a Jacob Arneson brick?

*The Founding Master's long-awaited autobiography.

60 At this very moment Professor Dodo, the Egregious Professor of Oölogy (Nem Con) was dozing away in the back of a taxi entering St Gaderine's College. The driver drove slightly too fast over the sleeping policeman and jogged him* awake.

'If you write down my age followed by my age when I was a year younger,' he remarked quite out of the blue, 'You get a four-digit number, taking the square root of which gives you my house number.' After this oracular utterance, he fell silent again.

If this is true, how old *is* Dodo, and what is the number of his house in Mauritius Crescent? **H**

*Dodo, that is, not the sleeping policeman . . .

Chapter Four

The Fellows of St Gaderine's and their guests were making their way to lunch. 'There!' said the Steward as he laid down the food. 'Looks good enough to eat, doesn't it?'

61 'Good Lord,' exclaimed Dr Juniper-Berry as he gazed into the murky depths of the alphabet soup he had just ladled into his bowl. 'I have all the five vowels in here: A, E, I, O and U. Why, that's the whole set.'

'Yes,' agreed Yamamoto the mathematician, 'but you can't make much with just vowels.* However, with just an extra Q, T, N and S you could make EQUATIONS!'

'Yes,' rejoindered Juniper-Berry woodenly, 'but why should I if with only two of them I can make a tree?'

Which extra two consonants should he fish for in order that together with only the A, E, I, O and U that he already has he can make a tree?

Which tree? **H**

*The Dean disagreed with this remark, as he knew of several words composed only of vowels, for example: 'ai' (the 3-toed South American sloth) and 'aiaiai' (the roseate spoonbill). For further vowel words see Appendix 61.

62   'There must be many words,' opined Dr Juniper-Berry,' in which A, E, I, O and U each appear once and once only.' 'Such as NUCLEATION, MALFUNCTIONED and OVERHAULING!' piped up a heating engineer, suddenly looking through a window.

'MENDACIOUS! IMPORTUNATE!' cried PC Klepto as if in hot pursuit of criminals, 'NEFARIOUS and UNSOCIABLE.'

'EDUCATION,' sighed Miss Highwater, 'FAVOURITE, TAMBOURINE, ENCOURAGING and EXHAUS-TION.'*

'We've had EQUATIONS,' said Mr Yamamoto, 'but there are also NUMERATION and MENSURATION.'

'I see,' laughed Szklowski, 'that you have chosen words from your own areas of interest. Also EDUCATION, on Miss Highwater's list, is an anagram of a word which might well have appeared on PC Klepto's list; whereas IMPOR-TUNATE which *is* on PC Klepto's list is an anagram of a word which might well have appeared on Mr Yamamoto's list.'

Can you say what the anagram of EDUCATION is?

Can you say what the anagram of IMPORTUNATE is?

*In fact, many of Miss Highwater's charges were UNREASON-ING, UNMOTIVATED IGNORAMUSES.

63 'Then there are PNEUMONIA, RHEUMATOID, RESUSCITATOR AND INOCULATE', continued Dr Czang.

'ANXIOUSNESS, BRAINSURGEON* and BEHAVIOUR,' suggested Dr Baxter the neuro-psychologist.

'EXHUMATION, CREMATORIUM, PUTREFACTION and AUTOPSIED,' was the contribution of Sir John Sturgeon, Police Surgeon, uttered a trifle too loudly for comfort. 'And since we are doing anagrams, perhaps someone can tell me which part of the body is an anagram of another part?'

Can you?

*This is normally written as two words, but it was only a suggestion after all.

64 'ULTRAVIOLET and PERTURBATION,' twinkled Stars, 'and what I gaze at the heavens with: STUPEFACTION.'

'HOUSEMAID,' said Lord Birdseed tentatively, followed more inspirèdly by 'EUPHORBIA, GARDENIOUS and UNBEGONIA.'

'You can't have *UNBEGONIA*,' complained Miss Bathpale, 'there's no such thing.'

'If you saw the plant,' chimed in Lady Birdseed, 'you might be inclined to allow there was.'

'I think we should allow it,' was Father O'Bubblegumm's tolerant view. 'After all, do we not have "Help Thou my unbelief"? So why should Lord Birdseed not offer up a prayer "Help Thou my unbegonia"?'

Szklowski cleared his throat, and looked down into the remains of his alphabet soup. 'Since you are all so fond of AEIOU-words here are some from which the five vowels, A, E, I, O and U have in each case been deleted:

THRSD
XLTTN
PHR
CMMNCT
BNDRS
PRCRS
NFRGVBL

'Don't be too DSCRGD by the absence of vowels: after all, all the consonants are still there in the right order. Can you deduce what the words are?'

Well, can you? **H**

65 'There are indeed,' continued Szklowski, many words in which A, E, I, O and U each appear once and once only, but very few in which they also appear in alphabetical order. We all know of FACETIOUS and ABSTEMIOUS. But I'm sure that Mr Buttermilk's eyes might well be described as CAESIOUS, being bluey-green.'

'We mustn't forget ARSENIOUS, ARTERIOUS and BACTERIOUS,' chipped in Sir John Sturgeon.

'Quite,' conceded Szklowski, 'but I'll wager none of you is quick enough to find a word in which all five vowels appear once and once only, but in *inverse* alphabetical order.'

'That's not very *flattering*,' protested Dr Fisch, rising to the bait.

Can you think of such a word? **H**

66   'Of course,' said Eulalia Winterbottom to Tunku Varadarajan, 'your second name contains five vowels, all of them A's.'

'Tamil is a good source of names rich in the vowel "A",' replied Tunku. 'For example, the name "Anantanarayanan" has seven. But there are also many words we use in English having a preponderance of one vowel: "ABRACADABRA" has five A's.'

'BEEKEEPER has five E's,' announced Telephonopoulos 'and RETELEMETERED has six.'

'And ZOONOSOLOGY* has five vowels, all of them O's,' was the Dean's contribution.

*The study of disease in lower life-forms.

'That reminds me of the racehorse called Pota-tooooooooo.** Nothing could beat that,' mused Miss Bathpale.

Raising an eyebrow, Szklowski replied: 'If you look in the latest edition of the *COD**** you will find a food listed as containing six vowels, all of them "A".'

Can you say what it is?

**The horse's name was pronounced, not unreasonably as 'Potatoes'.

****COD: Camford Oversized Dictionary.*

67 'Of course,' commented Eulalia, 'both *Anantanarayanan* and *Abracadabra* are what I call "ogopogo-words", by which I mean that they can, like "ogopogo", be written in a circle with an economising of letters, thus:

```
        O
    P       G
        O
```

Note that you must start at the top and go clockwise. For example:

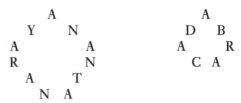

'Yes,' replied Szklowski, 'I saw just such a word in London recently. Perhaps you can guess what the word was.'

And he drew the following on his napkin with the tines of his fork:

Can you find the missing three letters? **H**

68   'Since some of us are about to start our second courses, let me serve you up with the following two ogopogic vegetables,' laughed Miss Highwater:

Can you say what they were?

69   'The following two ogopogics would be relevant to a musician,' suggested Mr Metal:

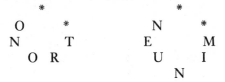

Which letters are needed here?

70   'And the following to a medical Doctor,' suggested Dr Czang, whose practice was on Potato Street:

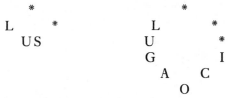

Can you prescribe the missing letters?

71   'Surely, ogopogic words are simply those which begin and end with the same letters in the same order,' reflected Baptiste. 'Well, I can certainly think of a few. In each of the following words you have to find the two letters which, when placed before and after the two letters given, will produce the whole word.' And he then scribbled down this list:

$$- - RI - -$$
$$- - CA - -$$
$$- - CI - -$$
$$- - CO - -$$
$$- - LU - -$$
$$- - NU - -$$

and:

$$- - IT - -$$

Can you complete the words? **H**

72   'Some ogopogics evidently have Roman numerals at their
      centre,' commented the Rev Eli Pet. And he elucidated with
      the following two examples:

$$- - XI - -$$
$$- - LIV - -$$

Can you supply the missing letters? **H**

73   'I think the most elegant ogopogics must be those in which
      just one letter is given,' said Szklowski. 'So for my contribu-
      tion I give you:

$$- - - X - - -$$
$$- - L - -$$

both of which would please the Rev Eli Pet, containing as
they do, Roman numerals at their centre.'

Can you supply the missing letters? **H**

74   'If it's elegance you're after,' ventured Drubchifel, 'try this:
      place the *same* letter in front of all these words and then the
      same two letters after all these words in each case making a
      new word;

$- OM - -, - YN - -, - ON - -, - IV - -, - OL - -$

then tell me which word is conspicuous by its absence.'

Can you tell him which word is missing? **H**

75   'Well as far as I am concerned, any way of economising on the number of letters we use would be a Good Thing.' Ray Dollymond spoke for the first time, and continued: 'The more we write, the more paper we use; the more paper we use, the more trees we cut down.'

'Yes,' enthused Eulalia Winterbottom, 'if we had only 13 letters in the alphabet, filing would take half the time it does now and typewriters would be compact enough to fit in one's briefcase.'

'You'll be asking us to write in Morse Code next,' muttered Birdseed.

'Well,' conceded Szklowski, 'the Hawaiian alphabet manages with just 12 letters: A, E, I, O, U, H, K, L, M, N, P and W.'

'Alphabet soup must be a bit of a bore for them,' muttered Birdseed.

'It doesn't stop them having long words, though,' was Cruddington's contribution. 'There's *humuhumunukunuk-uapuaa*, which is Hawaiian for a little fish.'

'It's certainly a big name for a little fish.'

'It reminds me of the little man who used to clean the windows at the observatory.' said Seymour Stars.

'How's that?' asked Tunku.

'Well, his name was Miles Long,' answered the astronomer.

'Another wasteful use of ink,' pointed out Dollymond, 'I can't believe it is necessary to use such absurdly long words, especially not for a little fish.'

'And if it were a *big* fish?' asked Luttgenstein.

'Of course, there are many long words in English,' began Szklowski.

'Yes!' shrieked Eulalia, 'Supercalifragilisticexpialidocious!' she chanted, which made Birdseed grip the edge of the table. Luckily she did not burst into song.

Szklowski resumed his theme: 'One springs to mind this moment: *floccinaucinihilipilification*.'

Mr Drubchifel, who had a weakness for collecting all interesting words, was moved to add:

'I can think of a 9-letter monosyllabic word with only one vowel and no Y's either.'

Can you tell what word he was thinking of? **H**

76 'It all depends, of course,' remarked the Rev Eli Pet, 'on what you mean by a "word". There is a distinction to be made between the written and the spoken word. For example, "ideality" is an eight-letter word of five syllables. On the other hand "breathed" also has eight letters but is monosyllabic.'

'If only,' commented Ray Dollymond, 'we spelt phonetically, long words could be long and short words would be short.'

'I mean,' continued the Rev Eli Pet, 'that adding a letter to a word can *reduce* the number of syllables in it. For instance, if I give you the letters F, T, A, B, I, Y and E you can make a four-syllable word. Now add one more letter in the right place and turn it into a three-syllable word.'

Can you find these two words?

77   'This,' sighed Father O'Bubblegumm, prodding his fish with a diffident fork, 'must be the piece of cod which passeth all understanding. I don't seem to be able to cut it at all.'

'Are you sure it's cod?' asked Tosher, 'It looks more like a sole.'

'Well, I'm not sure,' he replied diplomatically, still having difficulty cutting up his fish, 'for all I know it could be one of those humuhumuwhatsits, but what I do know is that there is a word in English with six vowels, all of them "I".'

'Just think,' observed Ray Dollymond, 'how much ink we could save by not dotting the "I's" in *that* word!'

No-one did think about this, as they were already busy trying to pinpoint Father O'Bubblegumm's word.

Can you think of it? **H**

78 'Well, *I* think the food is marvoulious and yumbacious,' said Homonininonymous heatedly. 'You should be jolly ger-grateful: you wouldn't dine any ber-better at any of the other colleges.'

'Not at Worcieworcester, at any re-rate,' teased Butermilk. 'I don't know what they served up at Old College last night, but I swear it tasted like roast mule.'

Leaving aside the aesthetic qualities of such a meal, can you find a single-word anagram of:

a) ROAST MULE
b) ROAST MULES?

79 'You will observe,' persevered Father O'Bubblegumm, 'that the vegetable accompanying this creation is not only *al dente*, but its name contains each of the five vowels once and once only.'

(a) What was the vegetable?

'Well,' said the Dean, 'since the *rest* of us are on the fruit course I think I shall choose of those two fruits which are anagrams of each other the one which occurs later in the dictionary.'

(b) Which fruit is that?

'What's more,' said Buttermilk archly, 'if you seek out yonder fruit-bowl you will espy a fruit the name of which contains all five vowels A, E, I, O and U.'

(c) What was the fruit the poet's eye had alighted upon? **H**

80   All eyes turned on Buttermilk's stance as he demonstrated to Mr Baptiste his dramatic talents. But he only got as far as 'Go pluck yon . . . ' when, to his chagrin, he was dramatically upstaged by the entrance of Chronos, left, carrying a Clock. There was a WHOOOOOSH, and a giant 'CUCKOO' reverberated around the room, sending ripples across the soup. At the far end of the table a fork stood on end and Dodo's hearing-aid shot out of the ear further from the sound and landed in Lord Birdseed's soup with a plosh. Not that the noise made had been an ordinary 'cuckoo'. According to Telephonopoulos, it was more of a 'cuckAEIOU': it did a sort of Cook's tour of the last vowel. 'Gosh,' he exclaimed, 'I've heard of the Camfordshire triphthong,* but that's ridiculous. That last conglomeration

*The local accent pronounces, for example, 'house' as 'he-au-oo-se.'

82

of vowels makes your cuckoo a *pentaphthongbird.*'

'What the devil's that?' grunted Birdseed, fishing Dodo's hearing-aid from his soup.

'It's a cuckoo-clock,' said Father O'Bubblegumm a trifle unnecessarily.

'There are,' expanded Mr Metal warily, 'several words in which vowels don't put in an appearance at all. You, Stars, ought to be able to think of a singular six-letter word without a vowel.'

'I can think of a plural one with seven letters,' countered Stars, 'which you, Mr Metal, with your love of music, should be able to deduce.'

'You whisper me yours, then, and I'll whisper you mine.'

What two words were whispered? **H**

Chapter Five

The Fellows of St Gad's and their guests then made their way to the Common Room for Coffee . . .

81   'Of course,' resumed Ray Dollymond, 'we would save much time, ink and paper – and many trees – if only we omitted to write all the vowels, as they do in, say, Arabic.'

There was a faint echo from the dozing Professor Dodo in the corner: 'Arrr – aaa – biiic . . . '*

'Oooh, I don't think *that* would be a good idea,' commented the Tosher, 'I'm sure a lot of ambiguity would result from *that.*'

'Ambiguity,' mused Dr Baxter, 'is the spice of life. Just think of all the CNFSN it would cause, not being able to tell the difference between a LOAF and a LOOFAH.'

'Yes,' assented Yamamoto, 'but although TWLV would be NMBGSL TWELVE and TWNT would be TWENTY, some NMBRS would be MBGS.'

WHT S TH SMLLST WHL NMBR THT CLD B MSTKN FR NTHR WHL NMBR? **H**

*According to Dr Baxter, this echolalic response was not necessarily of diagnostic significance: it probably represented the heightened suggestibility of the dozing.

82 (a) 'In some inscriptions,' Father O'Bubblegumm then pointed out, 'the vowels are indeed omitted, and the spaces between words left out. I wonder how many of us are familiar with the following improving piece of advice?'

And he wrote down in large letters on the back of an envelope for all to see:

PRSVRYPRFCTMN
VRKPTHPRCPTSTN

Given that the same vowel has been omitted throughout, can you make sense of it? **H**

(b) 'And in case you find that too easy,' added SZKLWSK, 'try this one:

DNSDNTGTLNDNNFTTSHPFRBKSRGWNS.'

Again, the same vowel has been omitted throughout. **H**

83   (a) 'I'm not in favour of spaces being left out, or the words left in, or whatever you want to call it,' declared Lady Birdseed. 'I, for one, wish to know whether I'm dealing with an archbishop or merely an arch bishop.'

'Or whether you're smoking a cigar with abandon,' said Buttermilk, 'or merely with a band on.'

'Punctuation,' Miss Corncrake stated boomingly, 'is to writing what stress and intonation are to speaking. I think you will find the following quite difficult to comprehend at first reading.' And she proceeded to write down these lines:

SMITH WHERE JONES
HAD HAD HAD HAD HAD HAD HAD
HAD HAD HAD HAD
THE EXAMINERS APPROVAL

'Yes,' observed Dr Baxter, 'and even when you've grasped what it says, it's ambiguous.'

Can you demonstrate the ambiguity by punctuating it and making sense of it? **H**

(b) 'As for hyphens,' warbled the Tosher, 'they are such useful little treasures.'

'Indispensable,' assented Eric Barendt, the law don, 'I should hate my brothers in law to become my brothers-in-law.'*

'Without it,' said Father O'Bubblegumm, 'how ever should I have written my sermon: "The -ism is theism; the -ology theology"?'

'When I read,' stated Luttgenstein, 'I want what I read to be readily understandable. I want to puzzle over what the author means, not what he is saying.'

*And, presumably, vice versa.

'In the deep sea,' intoned Mr Buttermilk, 'the fish don't see the water.'**

'Yes,' agreed Sir Freddy, 'who wants to be confronted with:

THAT THAT IS IS THAT THAT IS NOT IS
NOT THAT THAT IS IS NOT THAT THAT IS
NOT THAT THAT IS NOT IS NOT THAT THAT
IS IS NOT THAT IT IT IS?

Can you punctuate it so that Luttgenstein can get to grips with what it means?

**Buttermilk's arch paraphrasing of Luttgenstein's concern with the message rather than the medium presumably means to suggest that in the deep sea fish take the water so much for granted, they do not see it, only what is in it.

(c) 'I shouldn't like to see the dots vanish off the Boötes,'* twinkled Stars.

'Or the two dots off the Brontës,' added the Tosher, 'even if it *would* mean using less ink.'

'Well,' retorted Dollymond 'at least if they were abolished, it would stop Professor Dodo over there from writing "coöperation" and "zoölogy"**.'

A faint echo glided over from the corner where Professor Dodo dozed on: 'aaa . . . eeerrr . . . o . . . plll . . . aanne . . . '

'I remember,' recalled Birdseed, 'tearing spots off the signpainter I had got up from the Pig and Whistle to paint Chloë's name over her sty when he left the two dots off her name.'

*Boötes: (from the ancient Greek for 'herdsman') a northern constellation of stars the brightest of which, Boötes, is Arcturus.

**Dodo is unashamedly old-fashioned and uses the diaeresis (¨) whenever possible. When asked if he would like to fly, he is said to have replied, 'If God had meant us to fly he would have given us aëroplanes'.

91

'Well perhaps you will find these two examples for punctuation apt,' said Szklowski:

THE SPACES BETWEEN
PIG AND AND AND AND AND WHISTLE
WERE NOT EQUAL

and:

(d)   THE SIGNPAINTER SAID
THAT THAT THAT THAT THAT
THAT THAT THAT
SIGNPAINTER HAD PAINTED
FOLLOWED WAS
CROOKED

84   'And what do you teach?' Father O'Bubblegumm asked Ms Corncrake.

'Oh, children,' she replied, 'I shouldn't want to teach anything else.'

'Yes,' he persisted, 'but *what* do you teach them?'

'Why, the three R's,' came the reply.

'Why indeed,' chipped in Dollymond, 'that must be a most confusing term,* considering that only one out of "Reading, Writing and Arithmetic" starts with an "R". Of course, if only we spelt phonetically, learning to read would be a doddle. So would spelling. Just think of all those teachers out of a job.'

'Teachers, young man,' boomed Miss Corncrake, 'will never be out of a job.'

'Then there are all those redundant letters such as the b in "bdellium" or the g in "phlegm". It would save wear and tear on typewriters and word-processors if we wrote "thru" instead of "through".'

*Again there was the echolalic response from Dodo: "A mmmost confusing termmm . . . Hhiii . . . llaarr . . . y."

93

'It is true,' conceded Szklowski, 'words seem to use more letters than strictly necessary. For instance, I can think of a five-letter word which would be pronounced the same if you left off the last four letters.' **H**

Can you say what it is?

85 'There'd be a few cross words over the crosswords if everyone spelt words just as the spirit moved them,' pointed out Father O'Bubblegumm.

'We'd still need dictionaries,' observed Drubchifel, 'though not to check spellings – just meanings.'

'Or to see if words exist,' added Luttgenstein.*

---

*For someone who claimed not to believe in the existence of reality itself it is odd to be concerned about this issue.

'Enormous books they'd be, too,' remarked Sir Freddy, 'with multiple entries for, say, "house",** to include Lord Belvoir's "hice", not to mention the afore-mentioned Camfordshire pronunciation of "he-au-oose",*** hardly the sort of economy Ray had in mind, I'm sure.'

'The only solution would be to standardise the pronunciation, which would prove unpopular,' remarked Lord Belvoir. 'People don't want to lose their regional identity. It would prove most divisive.'

'And ambiguity would multiply,' added Dr Baxter, 'as homophones become homonyms.'****

**Lord Belvoir was used to say 'gorn' for 'gone' and 'abite the hice' for 'about the house'.

***See Puzzle No. 80.

****Homonyms are different words spelt the same (e.g. firs, furs and furze); homophones are pronounced the same (e.g. pear, pair, pare).

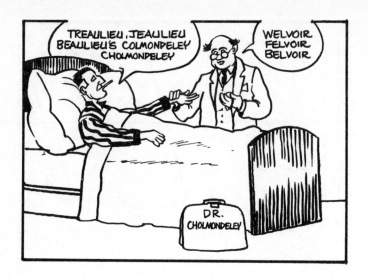

'English orthography is irregular,' conceded Szklowski. 'There are so many rules and exceptions to them it's often difficult to see which is which. George Bernard Shaw used to joke that Turner could be spelt PHTHOLOGNYRRH and GHRETI GHOTI might stand for FRESH FISH.***** Not to mention the spelling of Beaulieu, Cholmondeley and Belvoir.'

'Ah,' interposed Dr Baxter, 'but is that ridiculous spelling, or ridiculous pronunciation? And while you're thinking about that, can you find me eight words in each of which -OUGH is pronounced differently?' **H**

*****PHTH as in PHTHisis, OLO as in cOLOnel, GN as in GNat and YRRH as in mYRRH. GH as in enouGH, TI as in ammuniTIon and O as in wOmen.

86 'And what do you do?' Buttermilk asked Dr Baxter.

'Among other things I research into words dyslexics find difficult. One of the things I have to do is to search for and compile lists of words having particular features of spelling or pronunciation, two processes which are quite distinct. The previous puzzle involved pronunciation: going from what was written to what was spoken: from grapheme* to phoneme**, as we say in the trade. Now, spelling is the other way around: phoneme to grapheme. For example, the sound ERR has at least six or seven graphemic renditions.'

Can you find monosyllabic words in which the sound ERR is represented in writing by:

(a) UR

grapheme: a letter: i.e. the elementary unit of written language.

**phoneme*: the smallest sound identifiable in a word. For example YACHT has three phonemes: a Y-sound and O-sound and a T-sound.

(b) IR

(c) ER

(d) EAR

(e) OR

(f) OUR

(g) YRRH?

87   'You'll have to to come down to the Garlic Press,' piped up
      Drubchifel. 'I collect all sorts of interesting words on my
      card indexes. Acronyms*, homonyms,** homophones***
      . . . ' (At this point Telephonopoulos looked up; had
      someone mentioned telephones?)

      'Palindromes,'****   continued   Drubchifel,   'repeat-
      ables,***** hoity-toity words****** – you name it, we list
      it.'
      Can you identify the special feature about the words in each
      of these lists? H

      (a) DEVIL DOG LIAR REVILED FLOG PLUG
          FIRES DESSERTS
      (b) FIRST SIGHING CALMNESS HIJACK
          CANOPY STUN DEFT
      (c) ACCENT BILLOW CHINTZ JOY GNU
          FLOPPY

*Acronym: a word made up of the intials of others: e.g. radar.

**Homonym: see footnote to Puzzle no. 85.

***Homophone: see footnote to Puzzle no. 85.

****Palindrome: a word which reads the same when the order of
its letters is reversed: e.g. radar, rotator.

*****Repeatable: he means words such as agar agar and beri beri.

******Hoity-toities: he means words such as namby-pamby,
topsy-turvy and helter-skelter.

88   'Down at the Garlic Press we are constantly producing dictionaries,' said Drubchifel. 'Basic English, Pidgin English, American English, and English English.'

'Never had much time for dictionaries, myself,' muttered Birdseed, 'I mean if you don't know how to spell a word how the devil do you know where to look for it? Besides, how can you trust a book in which December comes before September?'

'And,' added Father O'Bubblegumm hopefully, 'life after death.'

'At the moment,' continued Drubchifel undaunted, 'I'm working on an anagram dictionary.* In the left-hand column is listed, say ADGHRSTU, and in the right-hand column: DRAUGHTS. On the left it'll say BEEEMPRST and on the right SEPTEMBER. In the left-hand column you look up: EEEELLNPSSSSS, and in the right-hand column you find – well, you tell me . . . ' **H**

Can you tell him?

*In an ordinary dictionary the words only are in alphabetical order. In an anagram dictionary the letters of each individual word are first sorted alphabetically before the words are.

89   'That sounds a very interesting invention,' commented Miss Bathpale, 'and one which could prove very useful to crossword addicts.'

'Never had much time for crosswords, myself,' muttered Birdseed.

'No, darling,' Lady Birdseed whispered loudly, 'you have time only for those awful pigs of yours.'

'Oh,' asked Birdseed defensively, 'and what's wrong with pigs?'

'They're *pigs*, that's what,' retorted Lady Birdseed frumptiously.

He knew better than to argue. Was there not something threatening in the use of the word 'darling'? Instead he tried to imagine that he could see Chloë's beloved face in one of the more abstract pictures at the end of the dining room.*

'There must be many double entries in your anagram dictionary,' remarked Szklowski, 'such as CHESTY, which will be paired up with SCYTHE.'

'Oh, certainly,' conceded Drubchifel, 'for example:

CARTHORSE TOENAIL PERCUSSION
OUTSIDE MARGINAL ELECTORSHIP

Can you find the word with which each of the above is twinned?

*Chloë was his lordship's prize sow. He often lay awake at night thinking about her. Lady Birdseed was used to say that only the quarantine regulations had prevented his bringing her along on their honeymoon.

90 'I *do* think it's a shame that the classics are no longer taught as once they were,' reminisced Ms Corncrake. 'They gave one a perspective on our culture as well as an insight into the way languages work.'

'Yes,' objected Dollymond, 'but just think of all that rote learning. And if you aren't a scholar, what use is it? The occasional phrase, an inscription. A clue to the origin of recondite words.'

'I still remember a *little*,' said Telephonopoulos wistfully. 'Nowadays saying Grace or acting as Dean of Degrees are the only ways I get to speak Latin. And if I were to crack a Latin joke, the younger dons would think it was I that was cracked. The same applies, *a fortiori*, to Greek. I wonder whether the assembled company can say what the following Greek letters have in common:

'It was Greek to me,' ventured Mr Baptiste.

What was the answer to Telephonopoulos's mysterious question?

91   'Well, I'm doing my bit,' began the Reverend Eli Pet. 'I'm rereading *Work and Days*,* which leads me to this rather apposite puzzle. Only one day of the week has a one-word anagram and it so happens that the anagram of the DAY has something to do with WORK. In fact, you could say that when I wake up first thing on the day in question, the anagram of the day is what I feel like.'

To which day is he alluding? And what is the anagram? **H**

*A book by HESIOD.

```
0.111111111111111111111111111111...
0.222222222222222222222222222222...
0.333333333333333333333333333333...
0.444444444444444444444444444444...
0.555555555555555555555555555555...
0.666666666666666666666666666666...
0.777777777777777777777777777777...
0.888         888888888888888888...
+  0.99        9999999999999999...
```

92 (a) 'I remember having to do that book,' recalled Belvoir, 'in particular that bit where the poet says "the half is greater than the whole". Which reminds me how much I hated decimals and fractions at school. Once, in later life, I fell asleep at the House and dreamed I was standing in front of a blackboard which stretched further than the eye could see to either side of me. In fact it was infinite. There was a sum written on it and the digits of the decimals repeated infinitely. I knew that no matter how far I went to the right I would never reach the last digit and so I couldn't even *begin* to add them up.'

'Well, that's really very silly of you, Lord Belvoir,' scolded Miss Corncrake, 'all it takes is a little *Commons* sense.'

What is the answer to the sum shown in Lord Belvoir's dream? (See picture.) **H**

(b) Lord Belvoir was the pride and joy of his parents. They came to England from Odessa with a Circus and never left. 'Now look at our boy – a legislator, no less . . . ' Which is a bit of a coincidence, as the word LEGISLATOR can be made by jumbling together the first names of his parents.

What are his parents' first names?

93 (a) 'And how are things in the Land of the Rising Pun?'
Szklowski asked Mr Triode, the editor of the *Camford
Journal*. 'Any more ambiguous headlines slipped through
the editorial net?'

'I assume you are referring to POLICE FOUND DRUNK
IN ALLEY,' answered Triode ruefully. 'Headlines have to
be brief, pithy and terse to be eye-catching. It's an economy
which carries the attendant risk of ambiguity. And when
you're working to a deadline it's not always easy to spot it.'

'Well, *I* think it's very clever,' trilled Eulalia, 'how you
manage, week in, week out, to fit all those articles so exactly
together into the little spaces allotted so there's never any
space left over, and never any words left out.'

'I'll let you into a little secret,' confided Triode. 'Many
words have longer and shorter forms. For example,
CAVERN can be shortened to CAVE just by crossing letters
out; PREVENTATIVE can be shortened to PREVEN-
TIVE just by omitting TA. The same applies to the word
CLIMatES. If we're running short of space, we use the
short form; if we've oodles to spare, why, we use the long
one.'

Eulalia Winterbottom blinked.

Can you, by omitting letters only, produce from each of these a shorter word of similar meaning? **H**

UTILISE SALVAGE EXHILARATION
INSTRUCTOR DEVILISH FALSITIES

(b) 'Ah, yes,' interjected Drubchifel, 'they call them kangaroo words, because the longer word contains a smaller version of itself – a word of similar meaning – just like a little kangaroo in its mother's pouch. When you've finished Mr Triode's puzzle you may care to try the converse problem: the following are the *little* kangas, so to speak; and you have to find what their mothers are called. Remember, the long words must have a similar meaning to the short ones.'

PIES SATED IDLE AMIABLE INSTANTLY
CHARM BOUNDS

94 'All this talk about kangaroos makes me long for my holidays,' declared Eulalia Winterbottom, 'the only question is to which and to what and with whom.'

'Go to Clacton, my dear,' whispered Lady Birdseed quite distinctly, 'That's *your* sort of town.'

'GO TO OBLIVIA!' barked Professor Dodo, starting from his slumber, in a sudden, rare and brief moment of fitful wakefulness.

'Where on Earth's that?' the Steward asked him.

'I don't re-mmemm- berr . . . ' murmured Dodo, relapsing into deep sleep.

'I certainly don't fancy Encumbria,' grumbled Colonel Plantpott-Smythe, oppressed by the memory of carrying Ms Winterbottom's cases on his head through mile upon mile of the Suckafoottee Swamps.

'Last year,' ventured Miss Highwater, 'I visited an island. As I drove off the ferry I passed a sign bearing the island's name in English, written in block capitals vertically down the sign. I couldn't help noticing that the name of the island read exactly the same when viewed in my rear-view mirror.'

What might the island have been?

95   'All this travel nonsense should be abolished,' grumbled
Birdseed. 'I'm sure Seymour Stars will tell you that all this
tramping about slows the Earth down or speeds it up, or
something. All this, "Go South, young man, and, while
you're at it, fidget-fidget, why not try South-South-East by
South-South-East of North-South-East followed by South
of North-East and don't forget to turn Left at Tapioca.'

'How odd,' said Miss Corncrake pointedly, 'if you take the
directions you mention, that is, six S's, four E's, two N's and
an L, and unjumble them you get a word which describes,
in your view, travel.'

What is the word? **H**

96 'I always let fate decide,' ventured Didipotamus, whose life was a pecurious blend of things causal and casual. 'Today and by chance, I opened a book left behind at breakfast by the Reverend Eli Pet. My gaze fell upon a single word in it: CASU – the Latin for "by chance". I say "single word"*, but my gaze was bifocalled and it appeared double. That is, I saw each letter exactly twice. Then I realised it was a sign from up there!' (At this juncture he jabbed his finger vertically into the air, just missing Lord Birdseed's flaring nostril.)

'Yes, if I unjumbled the eight letters – *Voilà*! My holiday predestination.'

Where is he (pre)destined to go?

---

*The company turned toward Dodo, but he remained silent apart from an occasional snuffle and snore.

97 'Wherever you go on holiday, do *not* go to Arbitraria,' advised Lord Belvoir. 'They are the most litigious people on Earth. An Arbitrarian will take himself to court if there is the slightest chance of successfully suing himself. Policemen regularly arrest themselves on the slightest suspicion.* I was fined for wearing brown shoes on Wednesday. The amount of the fine seemed quite arbitrary: you had to set your own fine, which you did (that Wednesday, at any rate) by using each of the ten digits 0-9 once and once only to make two whole numbers, the difference of which was to be your fine in Arbitrarian écus.'

'You mean like 965,438-1,702?' asked Sir Freddy.

'Just so,' replied Belvoir, 'except of course the rational thing to do is to try and make your fine as small as possible.'

What is the minimum fine in écus?

*According to Lord Belvoir this self-arrest is effected by means of mirrors.

98 'Well, since everybody seems to be going off in different directions, let me show you my new compass,' said Stars.

'Very fine,' conceded Colonel Plantpott-Smythe, who had done much exploring, 'but for one small detail. The East and West are the wrong way round.'

'Not for what I want,' replied Stars.

'I really can't think,' began Miss Winterbottom, 'why they don't move the Poles somewhere altogether more convenient.'

Szklowski looked puzzled.

'This could be achieved by swapping around lines of latitude and longitude. If they made them the East Pole and West Pole and put them somewhere on the equator, they could at once become more accessible and even profitable tourist spots,' persevered Eulalia. But Plantpott wasn't listening; he was wondering why Stars had had his compass designed with the East and West the wrong way round.

Can you see what he might have wanted it for?

99   'Talking of travel, does anyone know where the Isle of View is? I once received a *billet-doux* from there, confessed Juniper-Berry to Miss Corncrake with blushful sigh. He withdrew from his pocket a battered old card bearing the message shown below:

'Why, you dark horse, you,' trilled the Tosher, 'it's a rebus.'*

'What an odd name for it,' remarked Miss Bathpale.

'I suppose it comes from "*non verbis sed rebus*",** surmised Father O'Bubblegumm.

'Now, it depends crucially on the trees . . . ' teased Mr Buttermilk facetiously, 'is that a shoe tree?'

'Or a Beerbohm Tree?' joked Mr Baptiste.

'It's LMN-tree,' quipped Sir John Sturgeon.

Can you decipher Juniper-Berry's *billet-doux*? **H**

rebus – puzzle in which pictures replace words

**non verbis sed rebus* – not by words but by things.

100 'In days gone by we used such tricks to make our telegrams cheaper,' smiled Telephonopoulos, 'You know: "COMFORT ATONE – HAMILTON" would mean "COME FOR TEA AT ONE – AM IN HILTON." Nowadays that sort of trick appeals only to logo-writers and advertisers.'

'Is that the sort of economy of notation you had in mind, Ray?' asked Drubchifel, teasing Dollymond.

'We already have U-turns and T-junctions,' answered Helen Highwater.

'So why not snooker-Q?' asked Dollymond.

'And why not,' began Buttermilk, taking an enormous breath, 'A-zure, B-hive, C-side, D-bunk, E-longate, F-ervescent, G-hovah, H-bone, I-sight, J-walking, K-kmix, L-iminate, M-issary, N-ervate, O-ing, P-soup, Q-barging, R-gument, T-pot, U-tree, V-gan, W-rmoney, X-ellent, Y-rnetting and . . . ' (Here he switched to an American accent) 'Z-brugge.'

There was a loud cheer which was in danger of waking the Dodo.

'Well, if you're going to spell like that,' laughed Sir Freddy, 'then students will XL and have SA crises.'

'And PC Klepto will say LOLOLO,' observed Sir John Sturgeon, Police Surgeon drily.

'I suppose everyone is familar with:

YYUR
YYUB
ICUR
YY4ME?'

ventured Father O'Bubblegumm.

'If you're going to allow the use of numbers as well . . . ' interposed Yamamoto.

'Then a well-disposed dog,' interrupted Birdseed, 'can be a B9K9.'

'And we'll import oil again from Q8, just U8 & C,' was Lord Belvoir's effort.

'And we could have conversations like this:' said Dr Baxter, 'Have U810? Yes. I8MNXB4T – rather 2XSI fear.'

'We can get even further if we allow ourselves a few punctuation signs,' enthused Mr Triode, darting a sharp glance at Ray Dollymond. 'For example, can you decipher these words?:'

(a)   SP →   :EL   MU*D   NON+SED

    //engine   100-yard–   H&LE   F″

'It's EZ4NE12C,' I should have thought, burbled Buttermilk in a fake American drawl. 'S-pecially 4 me, grads/I/C!'

'That reminds me of the man with the donkey,' laughed Miss Corncrake, 'who wouldn't let his donkey cross the river because he had too good an *.'

'Before I leave you with one last puzzle,' called Szklowski, 'I'd like to say to Ray that I hope he writes down his ideas in a book. I'm sure it will make a good buy.'

There was a snuffling in the corner from Dodo, followed by: 'GOOOD-BYE . . . .'

The company including Dollymond burst into laughter and filed out of the Common Room leaving the Professor to his afternoon nap.

(b) Father O'Bubblegumm's puzzle:

There are many sequences of letters which with the ear of faith can be interpreted as words. For example, NRG = ENERGY, or TP = TEEPEE, or DFI = DEIFY. Can you think of a sequence of four letters with this property?

(c) A sequence of five letters?

(If you cannot decipher all the rebuses and puzzles in this chapter, a complete list follows in the Solutions.)

Chapter Six

The afternoon wore on and soon it was time for the Camfordites to take tea . . .

101 'The time is four o'clock,' announced Professor Turki as he put the petit-fours into the oven. 'Just time to solve this one:

'We need at least seven 4s to write the number 100 as a sum of numbers made up of the digit 4:

$$44 + 44 + 4 + 4 + 4 = 100.$$

We need at least sixteen 4s to make 1,000:

$$444+444+44+44+4+4+4+4+4+4=1,000.'$$

'Now, what is the smallest number of 4s we need to represent 1,000,000 in this way?' **H**

102 At a small birthday party in honour of Mr Telephonopoulos a cake was served. It was only a simple one-layer cake from the Bêtisserie Noir, but Monsieur Blancmange himself had iced it specially with the digits from zero to nine around the edge just like a telephone dial, except that the digits were all evenly spaced.

Now everyone present was on a diet and so, although everyone ate some, they all had portions of different sizes. The cake was cut in vertical slices radially outwards from the middle of the cake and although each person had a different number of digits on his portion, nevertheless the sum of the digits on each person's portion was the same.

How many people were present at the celebration and what fraction of the cake did each account for? **H**

103 Down among the filing cabinets in the backroom of 37a Selig's St. the dictionary-mongers of the Garlic Press were about to have their tea-break. As usual they were indulging in word puzzles:

(a) Mr Algenib was working on a dictionary of drinks. The name of his favourite drink is a word of nine letters among which are scattered the letters of its principal ingredient. Crossing out four letters reveals this principal ingredient. What drink? What ingredient? H

(b) Mr Algenib has two nationalities, both of which are anagrams of his name. What nationalities?

(c) Ms Schwa opened a bottle of tonic water, making a noise like 'SHCHA'. Of which word is – SHCHA – the precise middle?

(d) Find an anagram of TONIC WATER (6,4).

(e) Find single-word anagrams of a) DATE SUGAR
      b) GREEN TEAS.

(f) Find a single-word anagram of DICTIONARY.

(g) Of which words are these the precise centres?

a) – KLUS – b) – INEHE –

(h) Mr Algenib's book has 120 pages, numbered from 1 to 120 inclusive. How many times does a) the digit 1 b) the digit 0 c) the digit 9 and d) the digit 2 appear in the page-numbering?

(i) Drubchifel had a sense of *déjà-vu* when he saw the clock at tea-time. Both hands were on exact minute divisions, one separated from the other by exactly two minute-divisions. The same had been the case at breakfast except the hands were now the other way round. What were the two times?

104 Professor Tringle had baked a flat cake with three sides of
equal length and she asked Mr Tringle to cut it while she
made the tea. 'Now, mind that each piece be the same size
and shape!' she called out from the kitchen above the
whistle of the kettle. Mr Tringle cut it into four identical
pieces each having three sides. But he was supposed to have
cut it into three identical pieces each having four sides!

Given that he made vertical cuts only and the cake lay
horizontal on the table, can you show:

(a) How Mr Tringle cut it

and

(b) How he *should* have cut it?

105 Plantpott and Cruddington were lounging in cane chairs in the conservatory of the Old India and about to take tea when a football came crashing through the glass and landed in a hanging basket of flowers.

'In my day footballs were very dull things,' remarked Plantpott as Cruddington poured the tea. 'Two please. You had to lace them up.'

'Yes,' Crudders concurred, putting three lumps of sugar in the Colonel's tea, 'that one has curious markings though: black Tees.'

'It reminds me of a butterfly I once saw in Patagonia. . .'

But Plantpott had heard the Patagonian story in *all* its variants and he couldn't keep his mind on it. He wanted to know how many black Tees there were on the ball.

How many? **H**

106 'The places we've been! The things we've done!' sighed Cruddington. (For one fraught moment the Colonel thought he was about to be subjected to a rousing ditty) 'and now here we are twiddling our thumbs down at the Old India. It all seems like a dream now. Why, Samson, you and I have been to the ends of the earth, to the four corners of the globe.'

'I'm not quite sure that the earth *has* corners,' smiled Plantpott. 'But the compass has points,' replied Cruddington, 'N, S, E and W. All you have to do while I pour the tea is to place four of the principal points before the T and four of the principal points after it to make a word:

$$- - - - T - - - -.'$$

'That's easy,' cried the Colonel, reaching for the sugar bowl.

What was the word? **H**

107 Plantpott then told Cruddington about a cave in Outer
Monturkia where the explorer Potter had discovered a
triangular pattern containing 9 little triangles. He had
found that, all in all, taking into account triangles of all
sizes, these lines defined 13 different triangles. Deeper into
the cave he had found a second such pattern containing 16
little triangles. Taking into account triangles of all sizes,
how many triangles does that contain?

108 'I came across a similar phenomenon in Oblivia,' rejoindered Cruddington, 'except that the equilateral triangles* were marked out in dots rather than in lines.'

He made an illustrative sketch on the back of his napkin with the tines of his cake-fork. 'Now then, Potter, how many equilateral triangles can you find in that?'

*As Szklowski points out, an equilateral triangle is one with its three sides all the same length.

109 Testing the alibi of one Terence 'Fingers' Dactyl was
Q. C. Kewsie, QC. 'What time do you claim to have been at
the Dinosaur Club*?' he asked. Now Fingers not only had
difficulty telling the truth, but also the time (even though he
had done it once or twice already).

'I remember, beggin' yer Warship's pardon, that at the very
momint my person set foot through them hallowed port-
holes the big hand was exactly one minute ahead of the little
hand.'

Assuming that for once in his life, Fingers was telling
the truth and the big hand and the little hand were both
exactly on minute divisions, what time should the Recorder
record? **H**

*A practically extinct nightclub between the Lucky Gym and the
Achilles Heelbar in Soho. It is run by the O'Saurus triplets
(Tyrone, Dino and Rex) and is much frequented by the Opteryx
twins (Barry and Archie).

110 'Can you,' asked Telephonopoulos, 'by drawing two straight lines across this telephone key-pad divide it into a number of pieces in such a way that the sum of the digits on each piece totals the same *odd* number? The two lines mustn't cut across any digits of course.'

'How many pieces is that?' asked Stars, taking his pencil and ruler out of his pocket.

'Can't tell you that old boy, that would give the game away. But when you've finished that you can have a think about cutting this second keypad with two straight-line cuts in such a way that the pad is divided into three pieces. No cut must pass through a digit. The pieces are to be placed separately on the table in such a way that the sum of the digits in each piece gives the same *even* number.'

Can you say how each of these feats is to be accomplished?
H

111   The waitress in the Café Olé had lost track of the number of coffees and milkshakes consumed at table no. 17.

'How many had coffee?' she asks; fourteen put their hands up.

'How many had milkshakes?' Twelve put their hands up.

'How many had *both*?' Nine put their hands up.

Given that nobody had nothing and nobody lied or made a mistake, how many people were there altogether at table no. 17? **H**

112 Chief Inspector Dustcart arrived at his desk to find PC
Klepto waiting with the photostatic enlargements of
thumbprints he had asked for. He riffled through them,
shuffling them as he went. He counted them. 'Ten?' he
asked 'I only asked for nine.'

'Someone had left the photocopier on "two",' replied
Klepto. 'So you've got two copies of the first one.'

'First one?' fumed Dustcart. 'I've just shuffled them,
haven't I? Never mind, Klepto, let's approach this logically.
Two of the thumbprints match exactly; the others're all
different. I say "different", but they're so similar you can
hardly tell 'em apart. So instead of keeping 'em apart, we
superimpose two of 'em and hold them up to the light. That
way, any slight difference stands out like a sore thumb. If
they're the same, Bingo!, they match completely. All you've
got to do is start comparing them two at a time in the
manner your helpful Chief Inspector has just outlined for
you until you find the two that match.'

If Klepto goes about the task of comparing the prints
pairwise in the most efficient way, what is the greatest
number of comparisons he may have to make? **H**

130

113   Pembish and Punnish found themselves behind Miss Bath-pale at the fishmonger's which was apt to prove a lengthy business.

'Find me the two fish,' she said, pointing to a tray of smoked mackerel, 'which most closely approach each other in size and weight. They are for my two cats and I don't want them to squabble.'

While they were waiting for the fish to be weighed, Pembish started to think:

Suppose there are four fish in the tray and only and exactly two of them balance. You have an old-fashioned balance with two scale pans at your disposal. How many weighings at most will be necessary to isolate the two fish of equal weight from the other two?*

Well? **H**

*Assuming, of course, as Punnish would say, you do it in the most e-fish-ent manner.

131

114 Pembish had made the mistake of admiring one of Carmelle
Quantum's more abstract sculptures at an exhibition in Old
College. The thing arrived at Pembish Hall the very next
day in a crate marked 'Unicorn – Handle with Care.'

'It's a big cone,' Pembish pointed out as they uncrated it.

'A big con, more like,' grumbled Punnish who had little
time for modern art.

'Well this is certainly one "Unicorn" I wish didn't exist,'
sighed Pembish. 'But we can't just get rid of it. Its maker
may roll up at any time and expect to see it prominently
displayed in the grounds.'

'Well, if it's staying, I expect you'll be wanting me to paint it
with rust-proof paint, then?'

'According to my *measurements*, the radius of the base is exactly half the slant-height,'* mused Pembish. 'According to my *calculations* we shall need 173cc of rust-proof paint for the base of the cone, so all we have to do is work out how much we need for the rest of it.'

How could they determine the surface area of the cone without measuring it or knowing the formula for the surface area of a cone? How much paint is needed all in all? H

*The slant-height is marked S in the diagram.

115　Pembish had left instructions with Mr Zolyakar to make a side window in an outhouse of Pembish Hall. 'I want it to be a square and to measure 1 yard from top to bottom and 1 yard from side to side.'

Mr Zolyakar had agreed. But when Pembish arrived home from Camford he found the window not to be what he had expected.

'Well,' pointed out Punnish, 'it *is* a square, and it certainly is a yard across and a yard from top to bottom. But it only takes up half the area of the window you meant him to make!'

How had Mr Zolyakar done it?'

116 Pembish was making a cake. It was Punnish's part in this
enterprise to listen carefully to the recipe as it was given out
over the radio. Unfortunately Punnish, as always highly
distractable, told Pembish to add *five times as much flour as
butter* instead of *five pounds more flour than butter*. Punnish,
the one responsible for this mix-up, wasn't paying attention
as he was busy strumming a large wooden spoon as if it were
a balalaika. Fortunately the two quantities amounted to the
same thing.

How much flour and how much butter? (16oz = 1lb)

117 When Mr Drubchifel arrived home after a hard day at The Garlic Press, he challenged his son to tell him, with the exception of dight* and wight* – which he considered archaic – how many words there were in English of five letters that ended in the letters -IGHT.

Well? H

*According to the *Camford Outsize Dictionary*, *dight* means dressed; *wight* means person.

118 A weighing machine will not register a weight unless it weighs more than 16.5 kilos. A farmer had four bags of barley to weigh accurately but none would register singly. His son weighed them two at a time in all possible combinations obtaining the following results:

23, 26, 27, 28, 29 and 32 kilos.

'That's a lot of use, College Boy,' grumbled the farmer. 'Now tell me, if you don't mind, what each individual sack weighs.'

Well? **H**

119 (a) Mr Metal's son Rocco had spilt ink on the label of one of his father's battered old 78s. When Mr Metal put it on the turntable his head began to spin. Could *this* be his favourite composer? Why, the music issuing from the horn of the gramophone seemed almost *frivolous*. Then he realised his mistake: the first five letters of the composer's name had been obscured by an inky hand-print and the remaining letters happened to make the name of a composer of a date earlier than that of the true composer of the music on the record. Who was the composer of the music? **H**

(b) Mr Metal was unamused to find that the flipside label also had on it a huge ink-blot obscuring the first five letters of the composer's name, but this time leaving one of a date *later* than that of the composer of the music on that side of the record. Who was the composer of the music on *this* side of the record?

120 Didipotamus had one more calculation to finish before packing up for the evening. He had to multiply 142,857 by 71,421,283,542,495,663 and then divide the result by 999,999. Luckily he found a short cut.

What was the trick and what was the answer? **H**

Chapter Seven

As the day drew to a close . . .

121 Professor Didipotamus had one more calculation to make before taking Tanguy for a walk:

ABC - D - E - F -G - H - I - J = 100.

In the above each of the letters from A to J inclusive stands for a different digit. The calculation is, like all Didipotamus's work, quite correct.

What is the three-digit number ABC? **H**

122 When Miss Grammatica arrived home she found two
visiting-cards on her doormat. One bore the inscription:

ERICA CLIENT

and the other:

ANNE BAGMARK

'How strange,' she thought as she placed her ponderous
handbag on the hall table, 'they really ought to say what
their *business* is. It's as bad as that schoolteacher at St.
Awayday's whose card simply bears the name THERESA
CLOOCH!'

What were the occupations of her two visitors?' **H**

123 Father Dominic of St. Toad-in-the-Hole was trying to work out the number of hymn-cards he should buy. 'Now, there were 999 hymns in the hymnal at last count,' he reasoned. 'We have three hymns per service and the cards have numbers on one side only.'

'Ah,' said Father O'Bubblegumm, 'if you play your cards right and use the six as a nine and vice versa, that should reduce the number you need. After all, we are fallen on stony ground: even the bishops are economising these days.'

'Oh, I'm sure,' Father Dominic replied. 'And of course things would be even cheaper if we agreed to sing only certain of the hymns!'

(a) How many cards are required if the sixes and nines are not invertible?

(b) How many cards are required if the sixes may be used as nines and vice versa?

124 'The trick is to be mentally and physically alert,' PC Klepto told himself as he strolled down Lettsby Avenue with the rolling ease of a Samurai. Now I keep myself physically alert by doing lots of exercise and eating properly.* And as for mental exercise I do little calculations in my head. Like for example:

$$9876543210 = 999$$

Make that correct by inserting plus signs in the left hand side of the equation. There are two ways of doing it, of course, one being:

$$9 + 8 + 765 + 4 + 3 + 210 = 999$$

What's the other? **H**

---

*His favourite sandwich filling is cosh lettuce and truncheon meat.

125 At that very moment Mr Metal was watching a tiny fly
walking around the groove of a 78 rpm recording of The
Moonshine Sonata. Seen from above (the record was lying
flat on the floor) the fly was travelling clockwise. If she
carries on in this way, which will she eventually arrive at: the
centre label or the rim? **H**

126 According to Bertrand Russell, 'Mathematics may be defined as the subject where we do not know what we are talking about, neither do we know if what we are saying is true.' Professor Korinthenkracker Kugelbaum always knows what he is talking about, though few others seem to. He does not, however, always take note of who he is talking to. So it is a usual, if not regular, occurrence to find him sitting in a dark corner of the Maths Club talking to himself and contemplating out loud a few of the outstanding questions of the day:

(a) AB people each had BA pence. Altogether they had CD pounds. Now how many pounds was that? **H**

(b) How many whole numbers divide into 1,001 with the remainder 2? **H**

(c) How many whole numbers divide into 1,008 with the remainder 9?

(d) $\frac{1}{9}$ may be written as the sum of the reciprocals of two different even numbers in two distinct ways. One of these is: $\frac{1}{10} + \frac{1}{90} = \frac{1}{9}$.

What is the other way? **H**

(e) Single-word anagrams of GREAT NILS are TRI-ANGLES and INTEGRALS. What single-word anagrams may be made from GREAT NIL?

(f) If EAT + ATE + TEA = BUNS, what is BUNS?* **H**

*(U, N, B, A, S, T and E each stand for different digits.)

127 Carmelle Quantum, sculptress, dreamed she was painting
her latest masterpiece: a large cone. Acccording to her
dream 30cc of paint were required: 20cc for the curved
surface and 10cc for the base. But Ms Quantum, having
something deeper in mind, with a single cut parallel to the
base produced a mini-cone half the height of the original.
She discarded this, and decided instead to use the bottom
half.

When she woke up, she could not work out how much paint
she would have needed to paint the entire bottom half of the
cone.

Can you help her? **H**

128 The way Tomus numbers his collection of books speaks volumes for his eccentricity:

 8, 15, 22, 29, 36 . . . and so on up to 711, 117.

If these books were set out on one long shelf in numerical order, what would the number be on the spine of the middle volume? **H**

129 At present the last book in Tomus' collection is No. 711, 117. He adds books on to the end of his collection and continues the system of numbering begun in Puzzle No. 128 until the last book once again has a number consisting of nothing but 1s sandwiched between an initial and a final 7. What now is the number on the spine of his last book? **H**

130 Every 'bookend' number consisting of a number of 1s sandwiched between an initial and a final 7:

[77], 717, 7117, 71117, 711117 . . . and so on, has the property that subtracting the 2-digit number AB and dividing by the digit C gives a number consisting only of the digit C.

What are A, B and C? **H**

131 A hypochondriac, nervous of the approach of Hallowe'en, seeks out a full bottle of Soothing Mixture and drinks it until only a quarter remains. This leaves worryingly little, so he adds water until the mixture stands at the halfway mark. However, he soon realises that he has not increased the amount of medicine at his disposal, but merely diluted it, so he is relieved to find among his pills and potions a large phial of the same mixture, but $1\frac{1}{2}$ times as strong. He tops up the bottle with this and goes to bed. In the middle of the night he is woken by a nagging doubt:

Is the new mixture weaker or stronger than the original, and, if so, by how much?

132   Buttermilk had just finished writing a long-overdue letter to
       William McCandy who was on writer's retreat on a ranch in
       the midwest of the USA. But for the life of him he couldn't
       remember the name of the ranch.

'It was the name of a bird, I seem to remember,' the poet
told himself; 'perhaps if I think hard it will come to me.'

He closed his eyes, gripped the table as if at a séance and
emptied his mind of banal things.

'I see in a far land, atop a gate, a letter of the alphabet with
flames licking about it,' he called out.

What was the name of the ranch?

133 Pembish received through the post a belated Christmas present from the absent-minded Professor Kugelbaum: a diary for 1940. 'Better late than never,' thought Pembish. 'It's no good for 1991. But as each leaf bears only the name of the month, the number of the day of the month and the name of the weekday, it will be next usable when all the days of the year correspond correctly with the days of the week.'

For what year will the diary next be usable? **H**

134 'It's the thought that counts,' thought Pembish. 'A diary of this sort but for 1881 would be reusable after six years (1887) and again after a further 11 years (1898).'

What is the greatest number of years one might conceivably have to wait for a diary to be usable again? **H**

135 Lord Belvoir was suffering from insomnia after a dream in which he dreamed he was back in Arbitraria. To distract himself, he set himself the task of finding the largest number he could make by multiplying two numbers together which between them contained each of the 10 digits once and once only.

What should the two numbers be? **H**

136 Lord Belvoir picked up the *Camford Journal* and read how the governor of the Iambic Isles, where poets have to flourish without the benefit of an Arts Council, tiring of the constant and malicious satire directed against his illustrious and all-too mockable person, imprisoned an eleventh of the men in his charge and a seventeenth of the women. There were, according to the article, 200 adults on the island. Now, why the devil didn't they give the numbers, thought Belvoir, instead of swamping us with statistics? As he dozed off again he couldn't help wondering:

How many women had the governor sent down for sending him up?

137 On Monday morning Cruddington was cursed by a Voodoo man on the island of Salonga. That night he dreamed that on Tuesday when he awoke he had shrunk overnight by one seventh of his height; that on Wednesday when he awoke he had shrunk by a sixth of his remaining height; on Thursday a fifth of the remainder and so on.

By Sunday morning, on his way to Church, he was 10 inches tall. Luckily, he awoke from this dream, but on waking he was surprised to find that the arithmetic of his nightmare had been quite sound (even if his sleep had not).

How tall was Cruddington (before he fell asleep)? **H**

138 On the eve of November 5th, Professor Kugelbaum dreamed he was standing in his pyjamas at the centre of a

vast Catherine Wheel. The alarm clock under his arm was just striking midnight. Its ticking filled him with a sense of foreboding and he began to run round the spiral track of the wheel away from the centre. Although he set off at a good rate, he soon slowed down to a trot, only to speed up again as he saw how long it was taking. At some times he ran, at others he walked, or even rested fitfully, finally reaching the outside edge at exactly noon. He realised that it had taken him 12 hours to reach the outer edge of the spiral.

However, no sooner had he arrived than he saw that the fuse to the Catherine Wheel had just been lit! In panic, he immediately turned round and fled back along the track he had just covered. Stumbling and running, he at last regained the centre of the wheel. To his amazement, the clock again showed that it had taken him exactly 12 hours to complete the entire length of the wheel's coils.

Is it true that (not counting the beginning and end) there must have been at least one point on the spiral track at which the clock had shown the same time when Kugelbaum passed it on the inward journey as it had when he passed it on the outward journey?

139 Mr Telephonopoulos had, much to the amusement of the rest of the dons at St Gaderine's, become obsessed with word processing as well as telephones. 'We'll have to rename him Discopoulos,' they joked. Lights flickered in the general offices late into the night as 'Discop' twiddled about with his Iron Lady, happy as the day is long. Trouble was, the day was not long enough and so he hired some help in the form of Mr Gigo.

But Mr Gigo went Gaga and made strange mistakes. One paper on Higher Order Vagueness was considerably marred by the appearance of every possible number of commas from 1 to 64. This did not perturb Discopoulos unduly. He found in the manual that it was possible to replace a definite number of commas by another definite number of commas. For example, the instruction (37,17) would cause the machine to sweep once through each page of text consecutively. Wherever it found 37 consecutive commas it would replace them by 17 commas. This instruction would also affect any number of consecutive commas *greater* than 37: e.g. 42 commas would become 22 (the first 37 of them being replaced by 17, leaving $17 + 5 = 22$). Of course it would be possible to apply the set of instructions (64,1), (63,1), (62,1) . . . (2,1), a process consisting of 63 operations: a lot of good processing time wasted. What is the most economical set of instructions? **H**

140   It would be a little time before it became dark enough to use his new telescope, so Stars amused himself by turning it on the town. He watched people hurrying home along the streets and the newspaper-seller pacing to and fro in front of the shops. Suddenly his attention was caught by a flashing neon sign. What he saw was this:

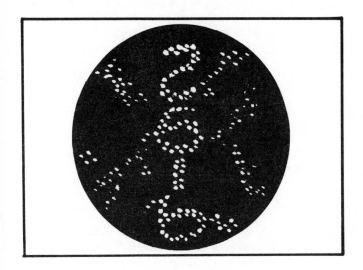

'What an odd number,' he mused. 'Well, actually, it's not *odd* at all, it's *even*.'

It was only as it grew dark that it dawned upon him that it was not an even number: in fact it was not even a number.

What was it?

Hints

1   The only possible way of having a birthday only once every four years is to be born on February 29th (i.e. in a leap year). But if one is born in February, how can one be born in March?

2   Only leap years contain a February 29th. Years whose numbers are divisible by four are leap years unless they end in -00, in which case they must be divisible by 400 to qualify.

4   The fewest number of years you can fit four consecutive ages into is three.

6   If a boy has as many brothers as sisters the boys are one up on the girls.

7   Either none, three or six of the children are triplets. Look for seven whole numbers which multiply together to give 6591.

8   Imaginative use of the dateline could come in handy here.

9   Pretend there is a replica Pembish as far behind the wall as the real Pembish is in front. A little reflection should then lead you to the right answer.

10   Despite the shaky start to his birthdays Uncle Percy lived a vigorous life and was never off his oats.

12   Try dropping a light letter or a sheet of card from a height and see what happens to it.

13   If it were *square* it would measure 4×4. But it's *not* square, so one side must be less than 4, one more than 4.

14   Pembish started both timers simultaneously and put the egg into the water when the 4-minute timer had just run out. Can you take it from there?

15   You either know this or you don't, which is not as tautological as it sounds. If you don't know, try spinning a hard-boiled egg and an unboiled egg.

16   It is easy to place three points equidistant from each other on a piece of paper. But where to put the fourth?

18   Plan A: Cutting off a corner adds three edges and one face. Plan B: Imagine a fly walking around each of the triangle's edges in turn. When she has covered the edges of each triangle once she will have covered all the edges of gatepost B once. She will also have passed through each vertex of gatepost B twice . . .

20   If anagrams are more your forte, the answer is an anagram of DON HEARD CODE.

21   The chances are not $\frac{1}{2}$. The chances of withdrawing two whites are 50%; the chances of withdrawing two blacks cannot *also* be 50%, or the chances of withdrawing either a white pair or a black pair (i.e. a matching pair) would be 50% + 50% = 100%, i.e. a certainty. But then there would be two white socks and two black socks so you couldn't be certain of withdrawing a matching pair: there must be a chance of withdrawing a white sock and a black sock . . .

23   Let the sum of the digits be S and their product P. Consider what the digits must be if P = 1, 2, 3 . . .

25   Pedants will note that the Camford town square is not a square at all but a stepped triangle. But, although it isn't a square and can't be rearranged to make a square, it *could* be rearranged to make a *rectangle*.

26   There is a connection between the number of zeroes at the end of a number and the number of times 5 can divide the number without remainder, i.e. how many of the number's factors are 5.

27   The number of pig snouts = the number of pigs, but the number of trotters is four times the number of pigs. So multiplying the number of pigs by the number of pigs by the number of sow's ears would have given a quarter of 128 = 32. If we had multiplied by half the number of sow's ears (i.e. by the number of sows) instead of by the number of sow's ears we would have obtained half of this. So the information boils down to saying that multiplying the number of pigs by the number of pigs by the number of sows = 16. Note that the number of pigs must be greater than the number of sows (since 'pigs' includes boars and sows).

31   The inspector couldn't make head or tail of the label. But then these aren't the only possibilities. A little *lateral* thinking may come in handy here.

36   Suppose the bill is for £ABCD. Then BCD×9 = ABCD. Start by finding D. What digit D, multiplied by 9 gives a number ending in D?

37   In the first part of the puzzle note that there is no requirement for all five triangles to be the same size. As for the second challenge, the stranger brought out a tube of glue.

38   Mr Zolyakar was standing in the middle of the Camford Town Square while he was trying to figure this out. See Puzzle No. 25.

39   No, it's not $\frac{49876}{50123}$.

40   The clue is in LANDOR.

41   Punnish considered buying both fruits in all three lines.

42    $1 \times 2 \times 3 \times 4 \times 5 \times 6 \times 7 \times 8 \times 9 \times 10 \times 11 \times 12$ is certainly divisible by all the integers from 1 to 12 inclusive but it's hardly the smallest such number. What is?

44   A fourteenth century date begins $13 - -$. But if you look at this in a mirror the 3 no longer looks like a digit at all. If you are still in the dark, a little reflection may lead you to another way of looking at this.

45   Count the pentagons first.

46   It would be gloomy to bemoan one's losses after a race. Far better to concentrate on how much is *left* after a race.

47    $0.125 = \frac{1}{8}$.

48   Father O'Bubblegumm saw that the diameter of each of the four little circles is half that of the big circle.

49   There are 10 ways of choosing the first volume. Once that has been chosen there remain nine possible ways of choosing the second, and so on . . .

51   Dikmas wanted WWWWBB but made BBBBWW, where B stands for a pint of black paint and W a pint of white paint. How can he reduce the *amount* of black paint?

60   Suppose Dodo was XY last year and is $PQ = (XY + 1)$ now. $PQXY$ stands for PQ hundreds and XY, and PQ hundreds is XY hundreds and one hundred. In other words $PQXY$ can be written as $XY00 + 100 + XY = $ a square $= S^2$, say. That is:

$$101(XY) = S^2 - 100 = (S - 10)(S + 10).$$

101 is a prime* number.
*Prime number: See Appendix No. 7.

61   The two letters Juniper-Berry needs to choose are among the four proposed by Dr Yamamoto.

64 DSCRGD is, of course, DISCOURAGED. The Police Surgeon calls these words in which only consonants remain 'disemvowelled words'. But then he would.

65 It certainly was *unflattering*.

67 The name of the thing is apt because it tells you where to find it.

71 Indeed! A

72 Eli Pet had seen these in his crossword that morning, corresponding to the following clues: 'Highpoints reached when mothers surround team'; and: 'Animate? Bet there is nothing muddled in it'.

73 'The four-legged followed by the two-legged makes the three-legged' was Szklowski's Sphinxian clue for the first ogopogic. The second is certainly Latin, but in the form of a *saucy* dance from South America.

74 Round about 199.

75 Giving up or cheating by looking up the answer would be *weaknesses*. What is required here is the very opposite.

77 Don't be cut up if you can't find this word at first sight. Walls have ears and potatoes have eyes; atoms, on the other hand, are un-cut-up-able.

79 (c) The fruit is harder than the vegetable, so here is a clue: an anagram of the fruit is QUIET NORA.

80 Use Y's instead of conventional vowels. Stars' word means 'a conjunction or opposition, especially of the sun and moon'. As for Mr Metal's word, an anagram of the countries TONGA and BURMA may suggest a pattern.

81 CFSN is, of course, CONFUSION;
NMBGSL = UNAMBIGUOUSLY;
MBGS = AMBIGUOUS;
NMBRS = NUMBERS.
The question is: WHAT IS THE SMALLEST WHOLE NUMBER THAT WOULD BE AMBIGUOUS?

82 (a) E is omitted throughout

    (b) O is the omitted vowel.

83 If you had had the education Smith had had (or was it Jones?) this would be easy for you.

84 That leaves just one letter. There are only 26 of these.

85 This question is quite tough though if you are thorough you should be able to see it through.

87 (a) These are not palindromes.

    (b) STU found this as easy as ABC.

    (c) Think alphabetically in order to solve this.

88 If you can't solve this straight off, don't lose any sleep over it.

91 The day is MONDAY.

92 (a) What is $\frac{1}{9}$ as a decimal?

93 (a) For example UtiliSE and SAlVagE.

95 In other words, an anagram of EEEELNNSSSSSS.

99 The first tree looks like a pine, the company eventually decided.

101 $100 = 44 + 44 + 4 + 4 + 4 = 4(11 + 11 + 1 + 1 + 1)$. So the minimum number of 4s required to represent 100 as a sum of strings of 4 is the same as the minimum number of 1s required to represent $\frac{100}{4} = 25$ as a string of 1s. Similarly the minimum number of 4s required for 1,000 is the same as the minimum number of 1s required to write 250 as sums of strings of the digit 1.

	11	111	111,111
	11	111	1
	1	11	1
	1	11	1
	+ 1	1	1
	—	1	? 1
	25	1	1
		1	1
		1	1
		+ 1	+ 1
		—	—
		250	250,000

For 250,000 we need ten 1s for the units place. How many for the tens column?

102 The sum of all the digits is 45.

103 (a) If you're stuck, try finding an anagram of THE COAL CO.

105 Compare this football with the one found earlier by Professor Kugelbaum in Puzzle No. 45.

106 If you can't see the light, an anagram of CANE CHAIRS may give a clue.

109 Q.C. Kewsie QC recommended trial and error. After all, the hour hand is only exactly on a minute hand every fifth of an hour, so the minute hand must have been on 00, 12, 24, 36 or 48. The hour hand can't have been far behind.

110 The digits sum to 45. Or *do* they?

111 How many had coffee who *didn't* have milkshakes?

112 If the first print doesn't match the remaining nine it can't be one of the matching pair can it? Don't forget, though, there may be a final twist to the tale.

113 Weighing fish to find the matching pair is a process different from the checking of one thumbprint against another as discussed in Puzzle No. 112. If fish A doesn't balance fish B we may not have found the fish that match but on the other hand we have found which fish weighs more than which fish.

114 Roll the cone around in a circle on the back lawn.

117 If you make it EIGHT think again.

118 As the 'College Boy' explained to his father, the two heaviest sacks must together weigh 32 kilos. Neither of them can weigh less than $15\frac{1}{2}$ kilos (why not?). Nor can they both weigh 16 kilos (why not?).

119 MR TED E. VINO, music critic of the *Banff Echo*, was so drunk when typing out an article on one of the composers that the name came out as NAFF BOCHE.

120 Multiplying *A* by *B* and dividing the result by *C* always gives the same answer as dividing *A* by *C* and then multiplying the result by *B*.

121 $ABC = 100 + (D + E + F + G + H + I + J)$. Also, $A + B + C + D + E + F + G + H + I + J = 45$ (the sum of all the digits from 0 to 9 inclusive). $(D + E + F + G + H + I + J = 45 - (A + B + C))$. So Didipotamus's equation may be written:

$$ABC = 145 + A + B + C.$$

122 THERESA CLOOCH is a SCHOOLTEACHER.

124 It is probably worth noting that the digits in the hundreds places add to 9 and the digits in the tens places add to 7.

125 Mr Metal knows which way a record spins on a turntable and what happens to the stylus when the record is playing.

126 (a) *CD* pounds is *CD*00 pence. $AB \times BA$ must end in -00.

(b) Suppose you have a heap of 1,001 coconuts. Dividing by the numbers we have in mind will always leave a remainder of two coconuts. Remove the two coconuts and deal directly with 999 coconuts.

(d) $1/X + 1/Y = 1/9 = (X + Y)/XY = 1/9$. So that $XY = 9(X + Y)$ and $XY - 9(X + Y) = 0$. Now, adding 9^2 to both sides: $XY - 9(X + Y) + 81 = 81$ and this can be written: $(X - 9)(Y - 9) = 81$.

(f) $EAT + ATE + TEA = 111 (E + A + T)$.

127 You can work out the surface area of the bit Carmelle kept by looking at the miniature conelet she discarded. (You don't need to know the formula for the surface area of a cone.)

128 First find the number of tomes in Tomus' collection. Note each book number is one greater than a multiple of . . . well, what?

129 Each book number in the collection is 1 + a multiple of 7. As Mr Yamamoto would say, each book number has the form: $1 + 7k$.

130 Since the result holds for all 'book numbers' no matter how long, choose a really long one:

$$7111111111 \ldots - AB = C \times CCCC \ldots$$

AB is small compared to $7111111111 \ldots$, so we can get good approximate results with

$$7111111111 \ldots = C \times CCCC \ldots$$

This is the same as:

$$7.1111111 \ldots = C^2 \times .11111111. \ldots$$

NB. $\frac{1}{9}$ = 0.1111111111 . . . (where the 1s go on for ever).

$7 + \frac{1}{9} = C^2 \times \frac{1}{9}$. So 64 = C^2, so C = 8.

133, Non-leap years have 365 days: that is, 52 weeks and a day.
134 Leap years have 52 weeks and 2 days.

135 Lord Belvoir found two guiding principles of use. The bigger the numbers the greater the product; so in the multiplication:

$$ABCDE$$
$$\times \quad FGHI\mathcal{J}$$

we want (*A* and *F*) = (8 and 9) or (9 and 8). (*B* and *G*) should be (7 and 6) or (6 and 7) etc..

The second was that if you want to divide a number into two parts which multiply to a maximum make the two parts as close to each other in size as possible.

137 Clearly Cruddington was $\frac{6}{7}$ of his height on Tuesday. What was he on Wednesday? On Thursday?

139 Initially all numbers of commas occur from 1 to 64. The range of commas is 1-64. We want to reduce this range. If we apply (*X*,1), what is the best value of *X* to choose? If *X* is 64 then all we do is reduce the range from 1-64 to 1-63, since (64,1) doesn't affect 63 commas. If *X* is 2 it leaves the range almost unchanged at 1-63. There must be some sort of intermediate optimum.

Solutions

1 Pembish was born in March, Cambridgeshire on February 29th and, since only one year in four has a February 29th, he has a birthday only once every four years. **A**

2 Punnish's grandfather was born on February 29th, 1896. Only leap years contain a February 29th. Non-leap years are those which are not divisible by 4 or which are divisible by 100 but not by 400. Thus 2000 will be a leap year but 1900 was not. So the next leap year after 1896 was 1904, the year in which Punnish's grandfather celebrated his first birthday.

3 Yes, there is no reason why one's maternal grandfather should not be younger than one's father.

4 It is possible only if today is January 1st and the man's birthday is on December 31st. **A**

5 The brothers could have been two of a set of triplets, the third being a girl. Equally, they could be the only boys in a set of quadr-, quint-, sext-, sept-, oct-, etc- uplets.

6 There are four boys and three girls in the family. Thus A has three brothers and three sisters and B has four brothers and two sisters. This is easily solved by trial and error but Erwigg Luttgenstein the philosopher prefers a logical and longer proof:

'If a boy has an equal number of brothers and sisters, boys exceed girls by one. So the number of boys (and hence brothers) a girl has must exceed by *two* the number of sisters she has. As the number of brothers she has is double the number of sisters, she must have four brothers and two sisters.' **A**

7 Six of them are triplets. For $6591 = 3 \times 13 \times 13 \times 13$. But we are looking for *seven* whole numbers which multiply together to give 6591. Since 3 and 13 are both prime numbers, the missing numbers must all be unity. That is: $6591 = 1 \times 1 \times 1 \times 3 \times 13 \times 13 \times 13$. **A**

8   Imagine being just west of the dateline just after midnight. Suppose that it is March 2nd (say). Wait for 12 hours until noon and the sun is at its highest point in the sky. Then proceed westwards in such a way that the sun remains in the same position relative to you. Then the time will remain, throughout the journey, noon on March 2nd. Since it takes the sun 24 hours to, as it were, circuit the globe, in just under 24 hours you will be just east of the dateline and it will still be 12 o'clock midday on March 2nd. Then wait until midnight and all in all you will have made March 2nd last 48 hours. It would work equally well for any other day.

As noted astronomer Seymour Stars would say: 'Any given day on Earth lasts 48 hours since as soon as you can find some place or other on Earth having a given date it will be possible during the 48 hours thereafter to find somewhere or other on the globe having that date.' A

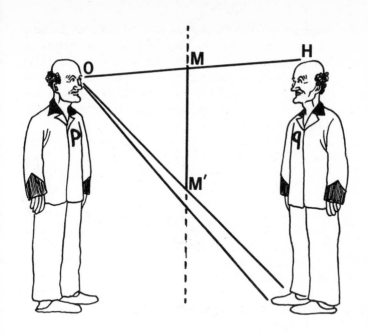

9   Pembish's mirror is 3 foot long and should be placed 1 foot 6 inches off the floor.

As Stars points out: 'If you look at yourself in a mirror it is rather like looking at an identical replica of yourself through a hole in the wall. The mirror, of course, corresponds to the hole. If you draw a line of sight from Pembish's eye to the top of the replica's head (along OMH) and from his eye to the foot of the replica (along OM′) it is clear that the hole in the wall must be at least half the length of the replica, i.e. half of Pembish's height. Actually the mirror must be slightly longer than this if Pembish is to see the tips of his toes.' A

10   Uncle Percy was a racehorse. Racehorses born in a given calendar year are reckoned as having been born on the first day of the year. Uncle Percy was evidently born towards the end of February or at the beginning of March.

11   Pembish drew an angle.

12   Experience shows that a letter dropped as in A) will flutter
      all over the place, whereas that in B) will sail almost straight
      down. Pembish forgot himself and released it as in A), as a
      result of which it fluttered into the flower-bed from which
      the postman retrieved it only with difficulty. Which only
      goes to show that a letter in the hand is worth two in the
      bush. **A**

13   The picture measured 3 inches by 6 inches and had an area
      of $6 \times 3 = 18$ square inches and a perimeter of $6 + 3 + 6
      + 3 = 18$ inches. Had the picture been square with side Y
      we would have $4Y = Y^2$ so that $Y = 4$. For all larger
      squares the number of square inches in the area will
      exceed the number of inches in the perimeter. For all
      smaller squares the reverse will be the case. So in order to
      find a suitable rectangle we require one side to be longer
      than 4 inches and the other to be shorter. A little trial and
      error along these lines results in a rectangle measuring 3
      inches by 6 inches. A less heuristic approach is to be found
      in the appendix. **A**

14   Let the four-minute timer be called A and the seven-
      minute one be B. Light the gas under the pan of water and
      start A and B simultaneously. When A runs out, invert it
      with one hand and with the other hand lower the egg into
      the already boiling water. When B runs out A has one
      minute to run and the egg has had three minutes. After A's
      minute has expired the egg has had in all four minutes and
      one minute's worth of sand has expired in B. Now turn B
      again and, when it has run out, the egg will have had, all in
      all, five minutes. The whole process takes nine minutes.

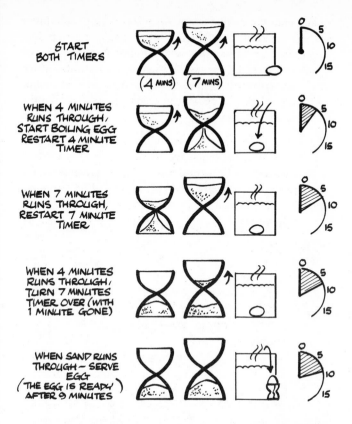

START
BOTH TIMERS

(4 MINS) (7 MINS)

WHEN 4 MINUTES
RUNS THROUGH,
START BOILING EGG
RESTART 4 MINUTE
TIMER

WHEN 7 MINUTES
RUNS THROUGH,
RESTART 7 MINUTE
TIMER

WHEN 4 MINUTES
RUNS THROUGH,
TURN 7 MINUTES
TIMER OVER (WITH
1 MINUTE GONE)

WHEN SAND RUNS
THROUGH - SERVE
EGG
(THE EGG IS READY
AFTER 9 MINUTES)

15 If the same initial rate of spin be imparted to a hard-boiled
egg and a raw egg, the boiled egg will spin more stably and
for longer. To sort eggs into hard-boiled and unboiled, you
could, in principle, give them the same intial rate of spin.
The unboiled eggs slow down dramatically while the hard-
boiled ones spin on stably.

However, the 'touch test' is more satisfactory, especially if
there is only one egg, or if they are to be tested singly. Set
the egg spinning, then touch it to bring it to rest, immediately removing your finger (from the egg) when it has done
so. If the egg starts to spin again rather weakly it is unboiled.
If it stays still it is hard-boiled. A

16 Each of three points can be equidistant from each of the other two if and only if they be arranged at the corners of an equilateral triangle. To place a fourth point equidistant from the other three and the same distance from them as they are from each other requires it to be placed in a different plane. Together the four points then form a regular tetrahedron.

Punnish could have done this by planting three seedlings at the vertices of an imaginary equilateral triangle and the fourth at the top of a mound between them. Alternatively he could have dug a deep hole in the middle of the three and planted the fourth at the bottom of that.

17 100. i.e. the chances of observing a palindromic reading are 1 in 10, or 10%. A reading is palindromic if it has the form ABA (where B could be the same as A). To find the number of such readings we need only note that there are 10 ways of choosing A and each of these may be combined with 10 choices of B. So there are 10×10 such numbers. The chances of such a reading are thus 100 in 1,000, i.e. 1 in 10 – not so unusual.

18 A has 36 edges and 24 corners; B has 24 edges and 12 corners.

(a) Cutting just a little off the corners of the cube adds 8 triangles and thus 24 edges to the 12 edges the cube already had, making 36 edges in all. Each corner snipped removes a corner of the cube but compensates by giving three new corners. So there are now $3 \times 8 = 24$ corners. Alternatively, as the mathematician Yamamoto puts it: 'Every vertex of proposal A can be assigned unambiguously to one of the 8 corner triangles and each triangle has three vertices so there are $3 \times 8 = 24$ vertices in all.'

(b) There are 8 triangular faces. Imagine a fly walking around the edges of each of these triangles in turn. She will have covered every edge once and once only. So there must be $8 \times 3 = 24$ edges. She will have passed through each corner twice and so there must be a half of $\frac{(3 \times 8)}{2} = 12$ corners.

Pembish so wearied of advice about the cubes atop his gateposts that he quite wilfully and arbitrarily had them replaced by wooden pineapples.

19 RECONSTRUCTING.

20 DODECAHEDRON – a body having 12 faces.

21 There is no chance at all of withdrawing a pair of black socks since there can only be one black sock. There cannot be four white socks or the chances of withdrawing a white pair would be 100%. If there were two white and two black the chances of withdrawing a white pair would be $\frac{1}{6}$, not $\frac{1}{2}$. To show this, consider the possibilities:

$W1W2$ $W1B1$ $W1B2$ $W2W1$ $W2B1$ $W2B2$
$B1B2$ $B1W1$ $B1W2$ $B2W1$ $B2B1$ $B2W2$

($B1$ and $B2$ are the black socks and $W1$ and $W2$ the white socks.) Of the twelve distinct and equally likely possibilities only two are a white pair so the chances are 2 in 12, or $\frac{1}{6}$.

Nor can there be no white socks or the chances of withdrawing a pair of white socks would be 0. So there must be three white socks and one black. **A**

22 The cable will wind onto the drum, and the drum will roll to the right as depicted in the illustration, i.e. towards the hand pulling the cable. Readers without ready access to a small

cable drum may like to experiment with a small reel of cotton. The effect works best if the cotton reel has a rim broad in comparison with the hub on which the thread is wound. The reel should be stood on a surface which is not too slippery or smooth. A gentle tension should be applied to the free end of the thread, which should be pulled horizontally.

23   The postman lived at No. 11 and there are at most 111 houses in Mauritius Crescent.

The smallest number having the required property has digits multiplying to 1 and adding to 2 (i.e. 11). The next smallest, whose digits sum to twice what they multiply to, has digits summing to 4 and multiplying to make 2. This must be 112. So there can be at most 111 houses on the Crescent or else there would be *two* house-numbers in it whose digits sum to twice what they multiply to.

24   She was fourth in a queue of seven. For if the man Miss Highwater had christened 'Bigears' went to the back of the queue there would be a) two more people behind than in front and b) twice as many people behind as in front. Removing the two extras would leave the same number in front as behind and halve the number behind. So there would be four behind and hence two in front. But Bigears didn't move, so there were three in front of Miss Highwater and three behind. A

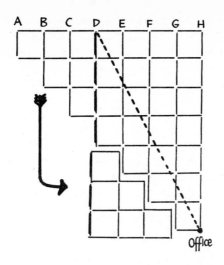

25   Imagine moving the six squares to the west of E down to the bottom of the square to complete the rectangle (see diagram). A straight line from E to the office bisects the rectangle. This means there is the same number of squares on each side of the line. But moving the 10 squares back whence they came does not alter the number of squares on either side of the line, so this line must be the bisector of Camford Town Square.

26   24 zeroes.

Only a multiple of 5 multiplied by an even number will produce a final zero. In the numbers from 1 to 100 inclusive there are more even numbers than multiples of 5, so it is the number of multiples of 5s that limits the number of final zeroes. Writing out the factors in turn: $1 \times 2 \times 3 \times 4 \times 5 \times 6 \times 7 \times \ldots \times 100$, we need consider only every fifth factor: $5 \times 10 \times 15 \times 20 \times 25 \times 30 \times \ldots \times 100$. Every one of these has 5 as a factor at least once, but every fifth (25, 50, 75 and 100) has 5 as a factor twice over. This makes 5 a factor $(20 + 4) = 24$ times, and this is the number of zeroes at the end of 100!.

27   Four pigs of which one is a sow. If the number of pigs be p and sows s, then $p \times 4p \times 2s = 8 \times p \times p \times s = 128$.

So $p \times p \times s = 16$. Now $16 = 1 \times 1 \times 16$; $1 \times 2 \times 8$; $1 \times 4 \times 4$; or $2 \times 2 \times 4$. The number of pigs must occur twice and must be greater than the number of sows. So there must be four pigs of which one is a sow.

28   MICROPHONE.

29   Suppose the weights are labelled 45gms, 50gms, A and B. Two of the weights ought to balance the 45gm weight. These must be A and B together. Another combination should balance the 50gms. This may as well be the A and 45gms. So A is 5gms. From this we see B is 40gms. Now we know what the weights are labelled.

The 50gms balances the 45gms and 5gms as it should, so the 40gm weight must be at fault. Since the 45gm goes down, the 40gm must be too light.

Dinge-Wittering is a sleepy hamlet with a corner shop and post-office selling, according to a misprint in the *Guide to Camford and Environs*, 'fire-biscuits and dogwood'. Unless the scales are repaired soon their reputation may be in the balance.

30   The title was what most of Buttermilk's poems generally are to him now: DISTANT MEMORIES.

31   The picture contained OXEN. The inspector couldn't make head or tail of it because both it and the notice had been hung sideways.

32   Goody-Goody cannot realise his ambition. To see this, suppose that each paper had been marked out of a hundred. Over the first four he must have gained 320 marks out of a possible 400. Over five papers he needs 425 to obtain an overall average of 85%. In the fifth paper he would need 105 marks. The best he can now manage overall is 84%.

33   There *must have been* 19 copies; there *may have been* 20 or 21: exactly the sort of nitpicking distinction relished by the best-selling author of *The Croissant from Argos-3*, *The Pedalo from Outer Space* and, of course, *Footpowder of Doom*. When asked by a critic why his latest tome is to be called *Chthono-*

180

nosologon McCandy told him, 'Because it sounds like a nail being tapped into wood.'

34   Her name was CAROLINE.

The two girls were named CAROLINE and CORNELIA because the letters from their father's first name and the letters from their mother's first name when jumbled up could be made to spell CAROLINE (or CORNELIA). Can you say what the parents' first names were? **A**

35   Chloë Nicolson (née Nicholson) and Cleo Nicholson (née Nicolson) – for these were the two talking through Father O'Bubblegumm's sermon – had each upon the death of her mother married the father of the other. Those that say God moves in mysterious ways should have seen Father O'Bubblegumm's efforts at breakdancing for the Steeple Fund Ball.

36   Mr Mayhem paid £375. The bill was originally for £3375, which is nine times as much.

To see this, suppose the bill is for £$ABCD$. Then: $BCD \times 9 = ABCD$. From this $D = 5$. So $BC5 \times 9 = ABC5$. Writing this sum out:

$$
\begin{array}{r}
BC5 \\
\times\ 9 \\
\hline
_45 = \quad ABC5
\end{array}
$$

Note the 'carry' of 4. So $4 + (9 \times C)$ must end in C, so C must be 7. $[4 + (9 \times 7) = 67]$, leading to:

$$
\begin{array}{r}
B75 \\
\times\ 9 \\
\hline
_675 = \quad AB75
\end{array}
$$

$6 + (9 \times B)$ must end in B, so B must be 3, since $(6 + [9 \times 3]) = 33$. Leading to:

$$375 \times 9 = 3375.$$

For a quicker method, see Appendix. **A**

The bill had been prepared on an electric typewriter and the 3-key was held down too long. At least, that was the wholesaler's story and he's sticking to it.

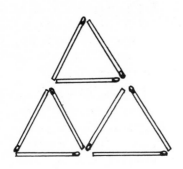 

37   Striker was more than a match for the stranger. He made a plane array. There are four small triangles and the whole array forms a triangle too, making five in all. (Note Striker did not say the triangles had all to be the same size). He then went on to make a 'double tetrahedron' as shown above, which contains nine matches and seven triangles.

38   In theory 28 slabs are required.
To see how it is possible to arrive at the answer without tedious calculation, as an act of what Mr Yamamoto calls 'intelligent laziness', see the diagram to puzzle No. 25, which depicts Camford Town 'Square'. The slabs of this square measure 1 metre square. The perimeter is clearly 28 metres and the number of slabs, each of area 1 square metre, is also 28. So this is obviously a solution. The question suggests that there is only one solution, so this must be it. It is.

To see that this is indeed the only solution, consult the appendix. **A**

39   69854/70123.

ABCDE/FGHIJ needs to be as close to 1 as possible so the top should be just less than the bottom. Since the fraction is the same as *A.BCDE/F.GHIJ*, we want the first digit of the numerator to be just 1 less than the first digit of the denominator. *BCDE* should be made as *large* as possible and *GHIJ* as *small* as possible.

40 Miss Grammatica suggested the names Arnold, Roland and Ronald, all three of which are anagrams of their surname: Landor.

The books Miss Grammatica was returning were: *Slimming for One* by Hugh Jelliphant, *Dinner is Served* by Carmen Geddit and *Wines I Have Known* by M. T. Bottle.

41 A pair of each must cost £2.00 + £1.60 + £1.20. i.e. £4.80. So one of each costs £2.40. Since a pineapple and mango costs £2.00 a starfruit must cost 40p. Similarly a pineapple must cost £1.20 and a mango 80p.

42 Stars' new number is 249480. It must have the form 24ABCD. Numbers divisible by all the integers from 1-12 inclusive must be a multiple of $11 \times 9 \times 8 \times 7 \times 5$, i.e. a multiple of 27720, written $m \times 27720$. Now m must be less than 10, since 277200 is larger than 24ABCD and more than 8, since 8×27720 is 221760. So m is 9 and Stars' number must be 249480.

43 The initial discs must be from top to bottom:

FBBBFFBFFB

Let the discs from the top of the stack downwards be numbered 0-9 inclusive. Discs 0, 4 and 8 must be F; discs 2 and 6 must be B; discs 1, 3, 5, 7 and 9 are skipped and put seriatim to the bottom of the stack so that we are left with 1, 3, 5, 7 and 9 in that order. Disc 1 must be B and disc 5 is F and 9 is B; 3 and 7 are skipped. Then 3 is skipped and 7 is F so finally 3 is B. This gives 0123456789 = FBBBFFBFFB.

44 1352. The collector had failed to realise the picture was also upside down. The date must begin 13 - -, but the 3 would look like an E in a mirror unless it were also seen upside down. 1, 3, 8 and 0 look the same when viewed upside down in a mirror, whereas a 2 becomes a 5 and vice versa. Since

the picture seemed 27 years older it must have said 1352 which appears as 1325 upside down in a mirror.

45 Kugelbaum was on the ball enough to realise that the far side of the ball carries 6 black shapes, so there must be 12 pentagons in all. There are thus 60 pentagon edges. Each hexagon requires 3 pentagon edges to define it so there are 20 hexagons. This assumes that the pattern on the ball was regular. But then, as Colonel Plantpott-Smythe pointed out, it would be highly irregular for it not to be.

46 Going backwards, which was what No Regrets just fell short of doing, Mrs Puttylump had three times as much before a race as after it. So she must have started out with $27 \times 50p$. Since 50p remained to her at the end, her overall losses were $26 \times 50p$, or $26 \times £\frac{1}{2}$ which is, appropriately enough, £13.

47 To multiply by 12.5 is to multiply by 100 and divide by 8. So divide by 8 (which can be done on sight) and add two noughts to the end. This gives:

$$1,020,304,050,607,080,910,111,200$$

48 400 square centimetres of blue glass. The area of the yellow parts equals the area of the blue parts. Father O'Bubblegumm can be sure of this because each of the small circles has half the radius of the larger and therefore a quarter of its area. Imagine the four smaller circles taken separately. Their total area equals that of the big circle. Their collective area is diminished by the area of overlap where they overlap. So the gap between the four circles and the circumscribing circle (blue) must equal the area of overlap (yellow).

If the priest wishes to places his faith in algebra instead, let the area of the circumscribing circle be C. The area of a small circle is $(R + 2Y)$ so $C = 4(R + 2Y)$. The area is also $4(R + Y + B)$, so $R + 2Y = R + Y + B$, whence $Y = B$.

49 There are 3,628,800 distinct ways of ordering 10 books (10 choices for first book, 9 for second, 8 for third etc, giving $10 \times 9 \times 8 \times 7 \times \ldots \times 3 \times 2 \times 1$ possible orderings.) As

one hot dinner a day is enough for any librarian this would suffice for almost 10,000 years.

50   231213.

51   He has six pints containing four pints of black and two pints of white: BBBBWW and he wants it the other way round, WWWWBB. Clearly, BB needs to be removed from BBBBWW which can be done by pouring off three pints leaving BBW. He should then add three pints of W giving BBWWWW. This way he only wastes three pints.

Commented the Rabbi: 'You need to remove two pints of black whatever you do. But this is mixed in with white. So the question is to minimise the wastage of white paint. Better you should remove the two pints of black in one go at the beginning when it is mixed in with as little white paint as possible. Any other procedure such as pouring a little away then adding white and then pouring away more and adding white again will not save paint.'

52   The careless assistants at the Rogues' Gallery had mounted the sculpture upside down. If you turn the book upside down it will be easy for you to see that there are four cubes, not just three. 'Of course,' snorted Ms Quantum, 'such a gaffe would never have occurred at the Museum of Imposs-ible Art.'

53   72 slabs.

Suppose a slab is one zgrod thick. Then the stack is six zgrods high, the breadth of a slab is three zgrods and the length of a slab is six zgrods. From this we see the volume of the stack is $6 \times 12 \times 18$ cubic zgrods. A single slab has 18 cubic zgrods. So the number of slabs must be $6 \times 12 = 72$. How many zgrods in a metre? It does not matter.

54    $4 \times 13 = 52$, as young Genghis realised from his card-playing (a pack of 52 cards contains 4 suits of 13 cards each).

55    $3 \times 54 = 162$.

56   Three kilometres from the punt-house is far enough. Suppose you set off downstream; your rate relative to the bank will be $4 + 2 = 6$ kilometres per hour. It will take you half an hour to reach your picnic site. After the picnic (add on an extra two hours) you still have $1\frac{1}{2}$ hours of your booking to get back to the punt-house, which is exactly how long it will take to travel three kilometres upsteam with a rate relative to the bank of $4 - 2 = 2$ kilometres per hour. Of course, it makes no difference to the answer whether you go upstream first or downstream, but most punters prefer to punt the $1\frac{1}{2}$ hour stretch upstream first to work up an appetite and then they have only half an hour punting downstream afterwards.

57   O rest a bit, for 'tis a rare place to rest at.

58   (a) There are clearly six patches each containing four smaller patches like abcd, and so there are 24 little patches.

(b) Consider a square patch. It has 12 T-junctions. There are six such patches and each T-junction is shared between two of them, so there must be 36 T-junctions.

(c) The Y-junctions all occur at the corners of the six square patches. There are six square patches each having four corners, but each corner is shared between three square patches so there must be eight Y-junctions.

59   The product of the three facial areas of a brick of dimensions A, B and C is $A \times B \times B \times C \times C \times A$, that is: $A \times B \times C \times A \times B \times C$. So the volume squared is $110 \times 52\frac{1}{2} \times 231 = 55 \times 105 \times 3 \times 77$, which is the square of $(3 \times 5 \times 7 \times 11)$. Hence its volume is:
$$3 \times 5 \times 7 \times 11 = 1155\text{cc}.$$
(To get the dimensions of the brick, divide 1155 by each of the areas in turn, giving 5 cm $\times$ $10\frac{1}{2}$ cm $\times$ 22 cm.)

60   If Dodo's oracular utterance is to be believed he is 82 and he lives at No. 91 Mauritius Crescent. ($8281 = 91^2$).

Mr Yamamoto's proof runs as follows:
Suppose Dodo was XY last year and is $PQ = (XY + 1)$ now. $PQXY$ stands for PQ hundreds and XY, and PQ hundreds is XY hundreds and one hundred. In other words $PQXY$ can

be written as $XY00 + 100 + XY =$ a square $= S^2$, say. That is: $101(XY) = S^2 - 100 = (S - 10)(S + 10)$. Now 101 is a prime number and cannot be split into factors* so either $(S - 10)$ or $(S + 10)$ must equal it. If it were $S - 10$, then XY would be 121 which is more than two digits.

So $101 = S + 10$ and S must equal 91. This should be Dodo's house number, and his age last year, XY, should be S -10, which is 81. His age now should be 82.

*Prime number: See Appendix No. 7.

61 If only Juniper-Berry can find an S and a Q in the soup dish he can add them to his five vowels to make SEQUOIA.

62 CAUTIONED and PERMUTATION. EDUCATION has the further anagram AUCTIONED, but that is not a very policemanly word.

63 ELBOW and BOWEL were what the gloomy Police Surgeon had in mind.

Can you find 10 parts of the body each of whose names contains just three letters? **A**

64 AUTHORISED, EXULTATION, EUPHORIA, COMMUNICATE, BOUNDARIES, PRECARIOUS, UNFORGIVABLE.

In case you found these too easy, Colonel Plantpott-Smythe came up with: RPTTN, MLTN, RGLTN, SBRDNT, BVCKD and MNVRNG.

Sir Freddy, the philosopher, produced: NCNSTRND, SPCLTN, DLG, XPSTLTNG, VRCS, PRSSN, RFTTN, NMPRTNC.

Cruddington suggested two qualities useful to the mountaineer:

MBDXTRS and TNCS

In each case all you have to do is add A, E, I, O and U to make the word. **A**

65 UNCOMPLIMENTARY was the word hinted at in the text. Other possibilities are: SUBCONTINENTAL, UNNOTICEABLY and UNORIENTABLY.

66 TARAMASALATA: a word in which As alternate with consonants. But, as Miss Pelling pointed out, the word TARAMA becomes TARAMO- in compound words, so perhaps the COD has been frequenting shady haunts!

67 UNDERGROUND.

68 TOMATO and ONION were the words Miss Highwater was serving up.

69 *ME*trono*ME* and *DI*minuen*DI*.

70 INsulIN and ANTicoagulANT.

71 DEriDE, DEcaDE, DEciDE, DEcoDE, DEluDE, DEnuDE, EDitED.

72 MAxiMA; ENlivEN. A

73 MANxMAN; SAlSA. Salsa is a Latin American dance incorporating elements of rock and jazz. For the ogopogic fiend here are a few extra:-

$$- - \text{UR} - -$$
$$- - \text{AT} - -$$
$$- - - \text{IZAT} - - -$$
$$- - - \text{SIOGRA} - - -$$

Remember, whatever letters you add in front of the word must be added in the same order after it. A

74 C is missing off the fronts and IC off the backs. The words are: COMIC, CYNIC, CONIC, CIVIC and COLIC. CUBIC is conspicuous by its absence. A

75 STRENGTHS is a monosyllabic word with only one vowel. Other monosyllabic words of nine letters include: STRETCHED, SCRATCHED, STRAIGHTS, SCREECHED.

76   BEATIFY becomes: BEAUTIFY.

77   INDIVISIBILITY.

78   EMULATORS and SOMERSAULT. **A**

79   a) CAULIFLOWER b) MELON (as a LEMON would be too sharp) c) ORTANIQUE. **A**

80   Stars had SYZYGY and Metal, as always, had RHYTHM. Metal was able to extend this to RHYTHMS, whereas Stars could not very well extend his word since its plural is SYZYGIES. **A**

81   THIRTEEN, which would be rendered THRTN, as would THIRTY-ONE.

82   (a) PERSEVERE YE PERFECT MEN,
EVER KEEP THE PRECEPTS TEN
was Father O'Bubblegumm's hidden advice about the TN CMMNDMNTS.

(b) DONS DO NOT GO TO LONDON ON FOOT TO SHOP FOR BOOKS OR GOWNS was Szklowski's sententious offering.

Both the above are univocalic: only one vowel has been used throughout. In the examples below a mixture of vowels occurs. Can you identify the unDollymonded version?

(i) TBRNTTBTHTSTHQSTN

(ii) And what about the following uniconsonantal, in which the vowels remain but the consonants have been removed: AEAAOOE? **A**

83   (a) Either:

SMITH, WHERE JONES HAD HAD
'HAD HAD', HAD HAD
'HAD'; 'HAD HAD' HAD HAD
THE EXAMINER'S APPROVAL.

or:

> SMITH, WHERE JONES HAD HAD
> 'HAD', HAD HAD 'HAD
> HAD'; 'HAD HAD' HAD HAD
> THE EXAMINER'S APPROVAL.

– interpretations with very different consequences for Smith and Jones. (There is also the possibility of its being EXAMINERS' and not EXAMINER'S.)

(b) THAT THAT IS, IS; THAT THAT IS NOT, IS NOT; THAT THAT IS, IS NOT THAT THAT IS NOT; THAT THAT IS NOT, IS NOT THAT THAT IS. IS THAT NOT IT? IT IS.

Which has to be one of the most prolix statements ever of the law of the excluded middle.

(c) THE SPACES BETWEEN 'PIG' AND 'AND' AND 'AND' AND 'WHISTLE' WERE NOT EQUAL.

Evidently the signpainter from the Pig and Whistle had a critical eye.

(d) THE SIGNPAINTER SAID THAT, THAT 'THAT' THAT THAT 'THAT' THAT THAT SIGNPAINTER HAD PAINTED FOLLOWED WAS CROOKED.

The effect of so many successive THATS is not unlike that of a mantra, as Dr Baxter pointed out, and numbs the mind. What the (first) signpainter said was:

'YONDER "THAT" WHICH YONDER "THAT" WHICH THE SIGNPAINTER OVER THERE HAS PAINTED COMES STRAIGHT AFTER IS CROOKED.'

The above is just that placed in indirect speech.

84   Queue.

85   TOUGH, BOUGH, THOUGH, THROUGH,
THOROUGH, HICCOUGH, COUGH, OUGHT.

86   BURN, TURN, SPURN, URN, BURR, CUR, FUR,
PURR, SPUR, FURZE, URGE, PURGE,
SPLURGE, SURGE, CURSE, PURSE, NURSE.

(b) FIR, FIRM, STIR, SQUIRM, FIRM, WHIRR,
DIRGE.

(c) PERM, FERN, STERN, TERN, TERM, ERR,
MERGE, SERGE, TERSE, VERSE.

(d) LEARN, EARN, EARTH, DEARTH, YEARN,
EARL, PEARL, SEARCH, HEARD.

(e) WORD, WORM, WORSE, WORST, WORK,
WORLD, WHORL, WORTH.

(f) SCOURGE.

(g) MYRRH.

The number of words to be found in each list depends on
the sample lexicon (the size and type of the 'wordpool'
you're fishing in). Polysyllabic words are more complicated

to deal with because the stress pattern in English can alter the way a given speaker pronounces the same word in different contexts.

87 (a) These each give a *different* word when written with the letters in reverse order. For example, GULP becomes PLUG. Such a word is called a HETEROPALINDROME, or, sometimes, a SEMORDNILAP.

(b) In each of these words three consecutive letters appear in alphabetical order. A word with four consecutive letters in alphabetical order would be GYMNOPAEDIC.

(c) Each of these words has its letters in alphabetical order. In Drubchifel's anagram dictionary (see next puzzle) these words will have identical appearances in left-hand and right-hand columns.

88 SLEEPLESSNESS.

89 ORCHESTRA, ELATION, SUPERSONIC, TEDIOUS, ALARMING and HELICOPTERS.

If you found those too easy, here are some more: TAPES-TRIES, TERGIVERSATION, COORDINATES, BANALITIES, DISORIENTATING, STAGNATION. **A**

90   The names of the letters sound like English words: beater, mew, new, pie, row, delta and iota. Telephonopoulos tells me that when he was at Stowe, when the names were called out at register the appropriate response was: 'STO' – meaning 'Here I stand'.

'Nowadays,' he says resignedly, 'people think Victor Ludorum is someone's name.'

If you found the letter question too easy or too difficult, you may care to say instead what was so apt about the remark uttered by the bardophilous Mr Baptiste. **A**

91   MONDAY; DYNAMO.

The puzzle was APposiTe, presumably because MONDAY is a day and a DYNAMO is connected with WORK. It is interesting to note that three months have single-word anagrams and that they are adjacent in the calendar. Can you say which months they are? **A**

92   (a) 0.11111 . . . , where the 1s go on *for ever* (i.e. without there being a final digit) is none other than $\frac{1}{9}$. Similarly 0.222 . . . without termination, or 0.2̇, as it is written for compactness, is $\frac{2}{9}$. In general $0.\dot{a} = \frac{a}{9}$. (This is easy to check by trying to turn, say, $\frac{1}{9}$ into a decimal.)

Belvoir's sum can thus be written:

$$\frac{1}{9} + \frac{2}{9} + \frac{3}{9} + \frac{4}{9} + \frac{5}{9} + \frac{6}{9} + \frac{7}{9} + \frac{8}{9} + \frac{9}{9}.$$

This is $\frac{45}{9}$, or forty-five ninths, which equals 5. For a proof that $0.\dot{1} = \frac{1}{9}$, see the Appendix.

It is possible to write a given decimal as a fraction in an infinite number of ways. For example:
$0.25 = \frac{1}{4} = \frac{2}{8} = \frac{3}{12}$ . . . and so on. Can you find just *two* different ways of writing the fraction $\frac{1}{2}$ as a decimal? (Final zeroes don't count; so, for example, 7.86 is the same decimal as 7.860.) **A**

(b) IGOR and STELLA.

93   UtiliSE, SAlVagE, ExhiLaraATION, insTrUcTOR, dEVILish, faLsitIES.

PastIES, SATisfiED or SATiatED, InDoLEnt, AMIc-ABLE, INSTANTaneousLY, ChARisMa, BOUNDarieS.

If you wish to try your hand at some more, here are some 'mother kangas':

FEAST, VARIEGATED, ASSURED; SPOIL; NOUR-ISHED,

and here are some 'baby kangas':

SKILL, WHIMS, APT, RUIN. A

94   Of the 26 letters of the alphabet, the only ones which when printed in block capitals appear unchanged when viewed in a mirror are those with bilateral symmetry:

A H I M O T U V W X and Y

Any name made solely from those letters written vertically downwards will remain unchanged when viewed in a mirror. For example, HAWAII, HAITI, TAHITI . . .

95   SENSELESSNESS.

96   The CAUCASUS. Naturally, when Didipotamus arrived there in his bifocals he saw two CAUCASUSES, which pleased him no end, since striking out the word CASU left him with CAUSES. He interprets this as signifying that those things which we attribute to CAUSES really occur by chance (CASU). When she heard this, Lady Birdseed snorted: 'Really Professor, you are impossible!' 'No, my dear,' he replied with measured condescension, 'just highly improbable.'

97   The minimum fine is 247 écus, given by 50123 - 49876. A

98   Stars wanted to fix the compass to the ceiling of his observatory on a rotatable platform in such a way that he could read it from below.

The word NEWS is supposed by some to have been made up from the letters designating the principal points of the compass. What is the longest word constructible using only letters denoting the four principal compass points? A

99   It says 'I PINE FOR YOU'. Juniper-Berry was evidently barking up the wrong tree, for he thought that 'Isle of View' was merely homophonous with 'I love yew' and that the card was from a fellow dendrophile.

100   XL = excel; SA = essay.

YYURYYUBICURYY4ME = Too wise you are too wise you be; I see you are too wise for me.

B9 = benign; K9 = canine; Q8 = Kuwait; U8 & C = you wait and see.

Have UE10 = Have you eaten?

I8MNXB4T = I ate ham and eggs before tea.

2XSI fear = to excess, I fear.

(a) SPARROW, COLONEL, MUSTARD, NON-PLUSSED, 2-STROKE ENGINE, 100-YARD DASH, HANDLE, FINCH(ES),

It's EZ4NE12C = It's easy for anyone to see. (Z is pronounced 'ZEE' in American.

S-pecially 4 me = especially for me.

grads/I/C = I oversee undergrads.
too good an * = too good an ass to risk.

(b) XLNC = excellency; FEKC = efficacy.

(c) XPDNC = expediency.

Which English county can be represented in this way as just two letters? **A**

101 43 is the smallest number of 4s required (See Hint No. 101). 250,000 requires ten 1s in the units column, nine 1s in the tens column (because of 1 carried over), nine 1s is in the hundreds column, nine 1s in the thousands column, four 1s to make 5 (with a carry over of 1) in the ten-thousands column and two 1s for the hundred thousands column (no carry-over). This makes 43.

102 The sum of the digits from 0-9 inclusive is 45. Now 9 is one of the digits; so the sum of the digits on each portion must be at least nine. If it were nine, 8 would have to paired with 1. But 1 cannot be paired with 1 as they are a non-adjacent parts of the cake. So there must have been fewer than five people present. Forty-five is an odd number; so there can only have been three people present. The sum of the digits must have been fifteen.

The digits on each portion must have been (7 & 8), (4 & 5 & 6) and (9 & 0 & 1 & 2 & 3). So the portions represented fractions of one-fifth, three-tenths and one-half (sic!) of the cake. Some diet!

103 (a) ChOCOlAte; (b) Belgian and Bengali;
(c) puSHCHair; (d) WINTER COAT;
(e) GRADUATES; TEENAGERS; (f) INDICATORY;
(g) LACKLUSTRE and SWINEHERD;
(h) 1 appears 53 times and 2 appears 23 times. Both the others appear 22 times; (i) Tea at 4:24 p.m. and Breakfast at 7:36 a.m.

104 Mr Tringle cut it as in A.

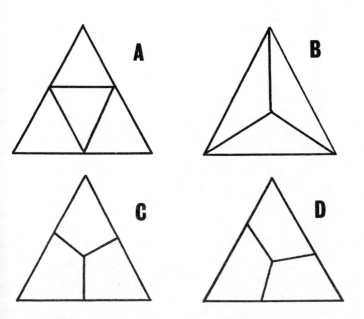

whereas he should have cut it as in B) or C)

But he could have cut it in all sorts of ways: D (these variants are obtained by rotating the three cut lines about the centroid of the triangle).

105 20 Tees. This ball has the same basic design as the ball found by Professor Kugelbaum in Puzzle No. 45: 12 pentagons interlocking with 20 hexagons in a regular pattern. As there is a Tee in each hexagon there must be 20 of them.

106 SWEETNESS. The anagram in the Hints is, of course, SACCHARINE.

107 There are 27 triangles in all: 16 little triangles of which ABC and BEC are typical; 6 triangles such as ADF, BGI etc; 3 bigger triangles AGJ, BKN and CLO; then there is the whole figure AKO, and the single upside-down triangle DFM. This makes 27 in all.

$$A$$
$$B \quad C$$
$$D \quad E \quad F$$
$$G \quad H \quad I \quad J$$
$$K \quad L \quad M \quad N \quad O$$

108 15 triangles: 9 triangles such as ABC or BCE; 3 triangles ADF, BGI and CHJ; the whole thing, AGJ; then there are also DIC and BHF. This makes 15 triangles in all. Potter found the last two the hardest to spot.

$$A$$
$$B \quad C$$
$$D \quad E \quad F$$
$$G \quad H \quad I \quad J$$

109 2:12.

The Recorder worked it out by trial and error. Clearly the minute hand must be on 0, 12, 24, 36 or 48 minutes after H o'clock, where H is yet to be found. Corresponding to these five possible positions of the big hand, the hour hand will be 0, 1, 2, 3 or 4 divisions after the hour division corresponding to H o'clock. We need only check five times: 11:00, 2:12, 4:24, 6:36 and 8:48 to see that 2:12 fits the bill.

PC Klepto did it in a more plodding fashion: if the time was H hours and y minutes, the minute hand points to y and the hour hand to $5H + \frac{y}{12}$. The minute hand is a minute ahead of the hour hand; so $5H + y/12 + 1 = y$ or $60H + 12 = 11y$. The left hand side is a multiple of 12 and therefore so is the right; so put $y = 12 \times k$, leading to $5H + 1 = 11k$. The left hand must be a multiple of 11 ending in 1 and H must be less than 12. So $k = 1$ and $H = 2$, leading to 2:12.

I think you will agree, the second method is a bit like hard labour.

110 The digits sum to 45 so the two lines must divide the pad into 3 regions, not 2 or 4. The digits on each piece must sum to 15. Stars suggested solution (A) for this.

In the second puzzle one of the pieces has to be turned upside down (B).

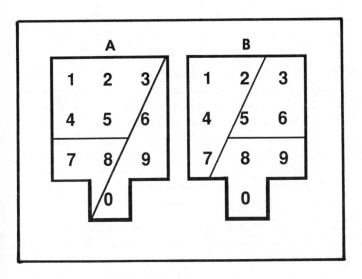

111 17.

Nine of the 12 milkshakers took coffee, so three didn't. All those who didn't drink coffee were to be found among these 12 since no-one drank neither. So there were three people in the party who didn't take coffee. As there were 14 who did, and you either drink coffee or you don't there must have been 17 of them.

112   44 comparisons.

Compare the first stat with the remaining nine. If it doesn't match the first thumbprint it is not one of the matching pair. Discard it, take the second and compare it with each of the eight remaining stats. The number of comparisons is clearly:

$$9 + 8 + 7 + 6 + 5 + 4 + 3 + 2 + 1 = 45$$

However, when we are down to the last two stats we have no need to compare them as they must, by elimination, be the matching pair. So at most 44 comparisons will be required.

The aficionado may like to produce the formula for the maximum number of comparisons necessary for a set of N stats of which exactly two are identical.

113   Four weighings suffice to isolate the equiponderous pair. Three weighings suffice to order three fish by weight. Compare two of them and call the lighter 'A', the heavier 'B'. Then compare the third fish with A. If C is lighter it will be the lightest and B the heaviest. However, if, instead, C weighs more than A, then A is the lightest and we need to make a third weighing to see whether B is heavier than C or vice versa. So three weighings suffice to order three fish. Suppose for the sake of argument the order is ACB.

If the pair had been among the three already weighed it would have been found. So D, the one which has sat it out up till now, must be one of the pair. Compare D and C (the fish intermediate in weight). Either it balances and D and C are the pair, or it is lighter and D and A must be the matching pair or it is heavier and D and B must be the matching pair.

114   Rolling the cone around on its side gives a circle of twice the base-radius and therefore of four times the base-area. Its circumference is twice that of the base and so the cone spins

twice on its axis in traversing the circle once. The area of the circle is thus twice that of the cone's curved surface, which is thus twice that of the base, requiring twice as much paint = 346cc. So altogether 519cc are required.

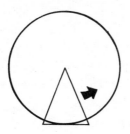

115   This is how Mr Zolyakar did it:

116   6 pounds 4 ounces of flour and 1 pound 4 ounces of butter ($6\frac{1}{4}$ pounds of flour and $1\frac{1}{4}$ pounds of butter). 5×1 pound 4 ounces = 6 pounds and 4 ounces = $5 + 1$ pound 4 ounces. ($5 \times 1\frac{1}{4} = 5 + 1\frac{1}{4} = 6\frac{1}{4}$.) The algebra of this question is

particularly simple: Let the number of pounds of butter be B. Then $5B = 5 + B$, so that $B = \frac{5}{4}$. The number of pounds of flour is $5B$ which is $\frac{25}{4} = 6\frac{1}{4}$. **A**

117 There are nine such words other than DIGHT and WIGHT. At first count Drubchifel had BIGHT, FIGHT, LIGHT, MIGHT, NIGHT, RIGHT, SIGHT, TIGHT. He accordingly answered EIGHT without realising that his answer was itself a 5-letter word ending in IGHT. He had probably missed it at first count because it is the odd one out in that it doesn't rhyme with the other words.

118 The sacks weigh 10.5, 12.5, 15.5 & 16.5 kilos. Let the sacks (from the lightest to the heaviest) weigh A, B, C & D. No pairwise reading is fractional. So sacks have weights which are either all integral or all half-integral.* **A**

Now, the 32 kilo reading could be the result of two identical 16 kilo bags; but then some of the readings would be repeated, which they are not. The only other alternative in which neither bag exceeds 16.5 kilos is that one weighs 16.5 and the other 15.5. So $D = 16.5$ and $C = 15.5$. The 29 kilo reading is due to $B + D$, so B weighs 12.5 kilos. The reading of 23 kilos is due to A and B. Since B is 12.5, $A = 10.5$.

*an integral number is a whole number, e.g. 3 or 1,089 or 12,345,679. A half-integral number is a whole number $+ \frac{1}{2}$, e.g. $7\frac{1}{2}$, or $99\frac{1}{2}$, or $1001\frac{1}{2}$.

119 (a) OFFENBACH; (b) MONTEVERDI.

120 $142{,}857/999{,}999 = \frac{1}{7}$. Dividing the number given by 7 is very easy as its digits are consecutive multiples of 7. So the answer is:

$$10{,}203{,}040{,}506{,}070{,}809.$$

121 $ABC = 140$.

$ABC = 100 + (D + E + F + G + H + I + \mathcal{J})$. The sum of the digits 0-9 is 45. So $(D + E + F + G + H + I + \mathcal{J})$ equals $45 - (A + B + C)$. Now ABC stands for $100 A +$

$10B + C$; so the calculation can be written in an equivalent but more illuminating form:

$$101A + 11B + 2C = 145.$$

If A were 0, $11B + 2C$ would have a maximum span of 115 ($B = 9$, $C = 8$): far short of 145. Since A cannot be greater than 1, it is 1. So $A = 1$, and $11B + 2C = 44$. So B is 4 and $C = 0$.

122 ELECTRICIAN, BANK MANAGER.

123 (a) 69 cards if 6 and 9 not invertible;

Zeroes are not used at the beginning of hymn numbers so six zeroes are needed (e.g. for 100, 200 and 300) and seven each of 1, 2, 3, 4, 5, 6, 7, 8 & 9 (e.g. consider the digit 7: hymn 777 and two 7s at most in the two other hymns).

(b) 64 cards if 6s and 9s are invertible.

Six zeroes are needed and seven each of 1, 2, 3, 4, 5, 7 & 8. Nine 6s: for 666, 969 and 999 for example. This makes 6 + 49 + 9 = 64. A

124 Note that in PC Klepto's example, the hundreds digits sum to 9 and the tens digits sum to 7. Any other arrangement of + signs such that the hundreds digits sum to 9 and in which the tens digits sum to 7 will automatically have the same units sum and hence also add to 999. One way of doing this is by increasing the hundreds digit of one number and decreasing that of the other by one so that their sum remains the same. This will automatically keep the sum of the tens digits the same, too:

$9 + 8 + 765 + 4 + 3 + 210 = 999$ (Klepto's example)

$9 + 8 + 7 + 654 + 321 + 0 = 999$ (our solution).

This, of course, turns out to be the only other solution. If, like 'Fingers', you find yourself with time on your hands, you may like to find the two ways of making:

$$1234567890 = 999$$

correct by inserting + signs only into the left-hand side of the equation. Of course, you're not allowed to move the digits about or anything suspicious like that. A

125 She will arrive at the outside first. To see this, note that when a record is placed on a turntable and plays from beginning to end it revolves clockwise as seen from above. Relative to the record, then, the needle moves anticlockwise as seen from above. If the needle (and hence, *pari passu*, the fly) were to move clockwise around the groove as seen from above, she would end up at the rim.

126 (a) £13. *CD* pounds is *CD*00 pence. So $A \times B$ must be 10 and so A and B are either 2 and 5 or 5 and 2. Either way, $25 \times 52 = 52 \times 25 = 1,300$. So altogether they had £13.

(b) Set aside the two whatevers that remain. The question then becomes: how many different numbers divide into 999 without remainder? $999 = 3 \times 3 \times 37 \times 3$; so the number of numbers is 7. (7 is the number of different selections you can make out of 4 things, three of which are identical). The numbers are: 3; $3 \times 3 = 9$; $3 \times 3 \times 3 = 27$; 37; $37 \times 3 = 111$; $37 \times 3 \times 3 = 333$; and $37 \times 3 \times 3 \times 37 = 999$. A

(c) The same procedure as in (b) above, with the proviso that only factors of 999 *greater than 9* need be counted; so the number of numbers is 5.

(d) $\frac{1}{9} = \frac{1}{12} + \frac{1}{36}$.
$\frac{1}{9} = \frac{1}{a} + \frac{1}{b}$. So $ab - 9(a + b) = 0$. Adding 9 squared to each side: $(a - 9)(b - 9) = 81$.
Now $81 = 1 \times 81, 3 \times 27$ or 9×9 only; so (a & b) must be (10 & 90), (12 & 36) or (18 & 18). In the last of these a is the same as b.

(e) ALERTING, ALTERING, RELATING, TRIANG-LE, TANGLIER, INTEGRAL.

(f) BUNS = 2,109.
EAT + ATE + TEA = $111 \times (E + A + T)$. $(E + A + T)$ must be greater than 9 as BUNS is a 4-digit number and less than 25 (since $9 + 8 + 7 = 24$). We also know that the last digit of the number $(E + A + T)$ must be S, since 111 times it = BUNS. So let $(E + A + T)$ = QS, where Q is either 1 or 2, and QS is less than 25. $111 \times QS$ = QQQO + SSS. Consider this last addition:

$$\begin{array}{r} QQQQ \\ +SSS \\ \hline ZYXS \end{array}$$

Q + S is added in the tens' column and in the hundreds' column. In the first case it gives X and in the second it gives Y. So there must be a carry involved. Q + S must be larger than 9. But Q is 1 or 2. If Q is 2 then S is 8 or 9. But QS must be less than 24, so Q can't be 2. So Q must be 1 and S must be 9. So QS is 19 and BUNS = $111 \times 19 = 2019$.

The letter Q was introduced into the solution for BUNS and TEA. Can you find a single-word anagram of the letters in BUNS, TEA and Q? **A**

127   The discarded mini-cone has $\frac{1}{4}$ the surface area of the whole cone. Therefore it would require 5cc for the curved surface. So the curved surface of the remaining piece requires 15cc. The base of the mini-cone has the same area as the top of the sculpture, i.e. $\frac{1}{4}$ of 10cc = 2.5cc. On top of that the base still needs painting: 10cc. So the sculpture requires, all in all, 27.5cc.

128   What middle volume? There are 101,588 books – an even number. There will only be a middle volume if the number of books is odd. To see how many books there are, imagine re-numbering each book by subtracting 1 from Tomus's number and dividing by 7. The new numbers will go:

$$1, 2, 3, 4, 5 \ldots 101, 588.$$

So there are 101,588 books. **A**

129   711,111,111,117.

Subtracting 1 from 7111 . . . 11117 and dividing by 7 must give an integer, so 7111 . . . 11116 must be divisible by 7. The 7 at the beginning and 11116 at the end are both divisible by 7 so we must insert the shortest sequence of 1s divisible by 7. This is 111,111 so the last number is now 711,111,111,117. **A**

130   The property holds for all 'bookend' numbers of the form 7111 . . . 17. Take a long one: 711,111,111,111. . .17. Subtracting AB leaves this unchanged except for perturbing the last few digits and must be arbitrarily close to $C \times CCCC$ . . . By inspection we find $C = 8$. Then choose a short bookend number: 77. We know that $77 - AB = 8 \times 8$, so $AB = 13$.

131   It is the same strength as the original Mixture. Suppose the bottle contains $4X$ grams of active substance. In the uncon-

sumed quarter X grams remain. Adding water does not change this. Half a bottle of mixture $1\frac{1}{2}$ times as strong contains $3X$ grams, so that after its addition the bottle again contains $4X$ grams of active substance.

132   FLAMINGO is the bird; FLAMING 'O' the ranch.

133   Non-leap years have 52 weeks and 1 day; leap years have 52 weeks and 2 days. January 1 advances one weekday after a non-leap year and 2 days after a leap year. 1940 is a leap year so the next 'useful' year must be one too, beginning on the same weekday. The 4-year cycle between successive leap years advances January 1 by $2 + 1 + 1 + 1 = 5$ weekdays. After N cycles the advance will be $5 \times N$ weekdays. To begin on the same day the advance must be a multiple of 7. The smallest such multiple occurs if $N = 7$, corresponding to 7 leap year cycles, i.e. $7 \times 4 = 28$ years. 1968 has gone now, so the diary is next useful in 1996.

134   40 years, i.e. 1888 – 1928 (NB: end-of-the-century years of the form $AB00$ are only leap years if AB is divisible by 4 without remainder, so 1900 was not a leap year).

135   96,420 × 87,531. **A**

136   4 women. (There are 68 women and 132 men on the island.) **A**

137   Cruddington was 5 ft 10 in (i.e. 70 inches) tall. He shrank to 60 inches, 50, 40, 30, 20 and finally to 10 inches. To solve this, note that Cruddington began as $\frac{7}{7}$ of his height. He then became $\frac{6}{7}$, then $\frac{5}{6}$ of $\frac{6}{7}$, i.e. $\frac{5}{7}$ and so on until the last day, when there was only $\frac{1}{7}$ of him left. It was on that fateful day that he felt, and was, only 10 inches tall, so he must have shrunk down from 70 inches, or 5 foot 10 inches.

Cruddington, as Miss Bathpale was quick to point out, was not normally a very regular churchgoer, but the regularity of his attendance improved markedly after the dream. But then, as Father O'Bubblegumm remarked, some people are only attracted to religion for the hell of it.

138   Imagine that as Professor Kugelbaum sets out from the

centre, a second Professor Kugelbaum, a Rosseforp Muableguk, as it were, is just setting out from the rim on an inward run. So long as they both start at 12:00 and both finish 12 hours later there must be a point on the track where Kugelbaum passes his antonym going the other way. Since they pass at the same time and the same place there must have been a point on the spiral track at which the clock showed the same time on both Kugelbaum's inner and outer journey.

139 The most economical set of instructions is: (33,1), (17,1), (9,1), (5,1), (3,1) and, finally, (2,1): six successive instructions in all.

The operation (X, Y) replaces X commas by Y commas. Whenever we replace a number of commas we may as well replace them by 1 comma as there is no point in replacing them by a greater number of commas than we have to.

To start with there are all possible numbers of commas from 1 to 64; we expect to find: , and ,, and ,,, and ,,,, and so on up to:

,,

that is, the range is 64. If we use the right value of X in $(X,1)$ we can contract the range. For example, (5,1) will contract the range to 60. The best we can hope to do with any operation of the form $(X,1)$ is to halve the range. To do this we need to apply the operation (33,1). Applying this logic successively with each new range gives the set of instructions given above. **A**

140 It is the word PIES written in a vertical column. He was looking at the reflection of a sign in the window of Harrington's pie shop. Astronomical telescopes usually turn things upside-down and do not reverse right and left. This means that if a bill sticker gluing up a poster sticks it up upside down it will read normally through an astronomical telescope.

The best way of seeing the answer is to hold the illustration upside down and look at its reflection in a mirror.

Appendix

1   Pembish's favourite composer, Rossini was born on Leap
    Year Day 1792 and died in 1868 round about his 19th
    birthday.

4   Four consecutive ages can be fitted into three consecutive
    years. The man has his 33rd birthday next year and there-
    fore his 32nd this year and his 31st last year. Since he was
    30 the day before yesterday, the day before yesterday and
    his 31st birthday must both be last year, since today is this
    year. So today must be January 1st and his birthday must be
    31st December.

6   Luttgenstein then came up with an algebraical proof:

    If the number of boys be $B + 1$ and girls $G + 1$. A boy has B
    brothers and $G + 1$ sisters. A girl has G sisters and $B + 1$
    brothers. Now a girl has twice as many brothers as sisters.

    $$B + 1 = 2 G \text{ (i)}$$

    and a boy has the same number of each, so that:

    $$B = G + 1 \text{ (ii)}$$

    Replacing B in (i) by $(G + 1)$ thanks to (ii) gives $G + 2 =
    2G$, so $G = 2$. The number of girls, then, is $G + 1 = 3$.
    Replacing G by 2 in equation (ii) shows that $B = 3$, so the
    number of boys is $B + 1 = 4$.

    Yet another proof runs as follows:

    Suppose there had been two boys and two girls: *BBGG*.
    Then a girl would have twice as many brothers as sisters.
    Unfortunately a brother would also have twice as many
    sisters as brothers, whereas we require him to have the
    same number of each, which means there must be one more
    boy than girl. Adding *BBG* will leave the brother to sister
    ratio unchanged for a girl and will also ensure that the boys
    exceed the girls by one. So *BBBBGGG* must be the answer.

    The disadvantage of the algebraical proof is that it is long
    and slower in this case than trial and error. But in general it

has the advantage in that it *proves* once and for all whether the answer is the only one possible.

Erwigg Luttgenstein was the sort of fellow who knew the difference between excursions in rain, excursions in the rain and excursions into rain, that is: rain (*the thing*), rain (*the substance*) and rain (*the fact of it*). * He had started out as a bit of a thisandthatologist, but had become involved with philosophy by chance, through the misunderstanding of an overheard remark. This led to his first paper, *Untürlichkeit*,** and finally to: *Religionsgeschichtlichnaturwissenschaftliche Untersuchungen*.***

7   A prime number is an integer (whole number) which has no other factors besides itself and 1. A factor is an integer which divides a number a whole number of times. For example, 2, 3, 4 and 6 are all factors of 12, but 5 is not, as it will not divide 12 and give a whole number as answer. 15 is

*Not to mention rain (*the nuisance of it*).

***When is a Door not a Door?* (Garlic Press).

****What there is*. (Garlic Press).

not a prime number since it has factors 3 and 5. But 3 is prime because it has no factors other than 3 and 1. Similarly 13 is a prime number because it has no factors other than 13 and 1.

Now every whole number can be written as a product of prime factors. To reduce a number to its prime factors replace the number by factors and the factors by their factors until all factors are prime. Since prime factors cannot be reduced further the process is then at an end. For example; $24 = 4 \times 6 = (2 \times 2) \times 6 = 2 \times 2 \times (2 \times 3) = 2 \times 2 \times 2 \times 3$. The same result is obtained however this is done: $24 = 2 \times 12 = 2 \times (3 \times 4) = 2 \times 3 \times (2 \times 2) = 2 \times 2 \times 2 \times 3$. It may be taken, then, that each number has exactly one representation in prime factors, not taking account of order, that is. So 6591 can be represented by prime factors in the form $3 \times 13 \times 13 \times 13$ only.

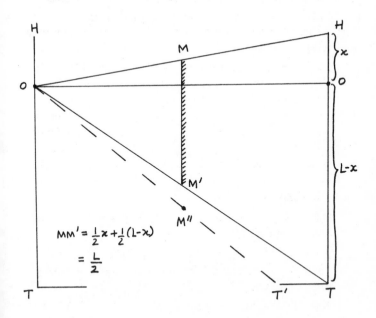

9   We don't know the vertical distance of Pembish's eye below the top of his head so let's call it x. His height is L. Assume

he doesn't need to see the tips of his toes. Then the mirror is half way between Pembish and pseudo-Pembish and has length $\frac{x}{2} + \frac{(L-x)}{2} = \frac{L}{2}$. This is independent of the position of Pembish's eyes. The height of the mirror up the wall is given by $\frac{(L-x)}{2}$, which *does* depend on the position of his eyes. But x is far smaller than L so an estimate will do. Put L = 6 feet and x = 4 inches. So the mirror needs to be 2 feet 10 inches up the wall.

The above assumes Pembish doesn't wish to see the tips of his toes. If he does, the mirror will have to be taller by an amount dependent on the length of his feet and also the distance he wishes to stand from the mirror. It will also have to be placed slightly lower on the wall.

12   The effect the air resistance has on the letter depends on all sorts of factors, such as how fast it is falling, how it was released and its shape and weight.

13   Let the frame be x inches by y inches. The area in square inches is xy and the perimeter in inches is $2(x + y)$. We require that xy equal $2(x + y)$. So that $xy = 2x + 2y$. Now $(x - 2)(y - 2) = xy - 2x - 2y + 4$, so we can rewrite $xy = 2x + 2y$ as:

$$xy - 2x - 2y + 4 = 4$$

hence:

$$(x - 2)(y - 2) = 4$$

So $(x - 2)(y - 2) = 1 \times 4$ or 2×2. Either $x - 2 = 1$ and $y - 2 = 4$ (in which case x = 3 and y = 6) or $x - 2 = 2$ and $y - 2 = 2$ (in which case $x = y = 4$). These are the only two possibilities, and since the frame was not square, it must have been $3'' \times 6''$.

15   A raw egg begins to spin again weakly after being stopped briefly. This is explained in terms of the (angular) momentum of the yolk floating within the white – once the yolk is moving it tends to keep moving even if the shell is stopped.

21   If there are four socks and W of them are white, the chances of withdrawing two white are $\frac{W(W-1)}{(4)(3)}$, which equals $\frac{W(W-1)}{12}$.

We are told this equals $\frac{1}{2}$ so $W(W-1) = 6$, so that $W = 3$. So there is only one black sock. Another way to see this is that if there were two black socks and two white socks there would have to be the same chance of picking a matching pair of either. But the chances of a white pair are $\frac{1}{2}$ so the chances of choosing a black pair would have to be $\frac{1}{2}$ too. But $\frac{1}{2} + \frac{1}{2} = 1$, so the chances of choosing either a white pair or a black pair would then be certainty. But if there are 2 white socks and 2 black socks there must be a chance of choosing a mixed pair. Therefore the chances of choosing two white socks being equal to $\frac{1}{2}$ is not consistent with their being two white socks and two black socks.

24   If the number in front and behind of Miss Highwater is Q, then $2(Q-1) = Q+1$; i.e. $Q = 3$. So she is the middle of 7.

34   They were ERIC and NOLA, though they could have been RON and ALICE (or CELIA), IAN and CAROL (or CORAL) or IONE and CARL.

36   Mr Yamamoto finds this solution more elegant than Mr Mayhem's: Let the sum be £$ABCD$. Then $ABCD = 9 \times BCD$, and, dividing both sides by 1,000: $A.BCD = 9 \times 0.BCD$. Now, $A.BCD = A + 0.BCD$. So $A + 0.BCD = 9 \times 0.BCD$, which is as much as to say $A = 8 \times 0.BCD$, so that $\frac{A}{8} = 0.BCD$. Now A is an odd digit, because we were told it was. So we know that $A = 1, 3, 5$ or 7. (It can't be 9 because $\frac{9}{8}$ is bigger than $0.BCD$). So we look at:

$\frac{1}{8} = 0.125$ $\frac{5}{8} = 0.625$

$\frac{3}{8} = 0.375$ $\frac{7}{8} = 0.875$

The only one which 'fits the bill' in that it has only odd digits is $\frac{3}{8}$. So $A = 3$ and $0.BCD = 0.375$, so £$ABCD$ = £3375.

38   If there are N square slabs along one of the straight sides of the stepped rectangle, the number of slabs is: $1 + 2 + 3 + 4 + \ldots + N$. This is equal to $\frac{N(N+1)}{2}$. So the area in square metres is $\frac{N(N+1)}{2}$ and the perimeter in metres is $4N$. If these are equal, either $N = 0$ (no stepped rectangle and no commission) or $N + 1 = 8$, i.e. $N = 7$ and the number of slabs required is $\frac{N(N+1)}{2} = 28$.

This assumes that the steps along the hypotenuse are of one slab only as implied by the picture accompanying the puzzle. If the steps are to be of the same size but no longer have to be of one slab, further solutions become possible; for example:

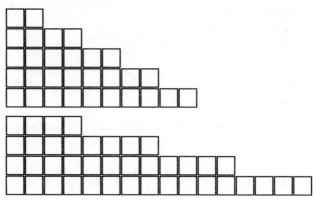

61 The Dean, Dr Kennel-Bark, disagreed with this remark, and produced the following rather recondite consonantless words: *ai*: three-toed sloth of South America; *ea*: a stream; *io*: a large Hawaiian hawk; also *Io*: one of the satellites of the planet Jupiter; *oe*: a violent storm or whirlwind of the Faroe islands; *iao*: the wattled honey-eater bird; *ioa*: the frigate bird. If repeated vowels are allowed: *aa*: a type of lava; *oo*: an extinct Hawaiian bird; *ieie*: a pine of the Pacific; *Aeaeae*: the fable home of Circe (now Mount Circello); *Euouae*: any trope, particularly that of the Gregorian Lesser Doxology. There are, of course, many more.

The trouble with consonantless words such as *o-o* or *o-o-a-a*, as Miss Highwater pointed out, is that they are apt to sound like the noises made by an imprudent diner who, in company, has too rashly inserted a whole, too ho-hot potato into the mouth.

63 EYE, GUM, RIB, LIP, TOE, JAW, EAR, HIP, ARM and LEG. Ms Winterbottom suggested LAP, but Luttgenstein argued that this was not really part of the body. After all, where did it go when we stood up?

64   The Colonel's words were:

REPUTATION, EMULATION, REGULATION, SUB-
ORDINATE, BIVOUACKED and MANOEUVRING.

Sir Freddy's were:

UNCONSTRAINED, SPECULATION, DIALOGUE,
EXPOSTULATING, PERSUASION, REFUTATION,
VERACIOUS and, finally, UNIMPORTANCE.

Cruddington's mountaineer should be AMBIDEXTRO-
US and TENACIOUS. There are hundreds of such
AEIOU-words in the English language.

71   For those unfamiliar with cryptic clues, the hint signifies
that each of the given clusters of letters is to be embedded in
DE – – DE(!)

72   *HIGHPOINTS* are *MAXIMA*. The two mothers are *MA*
and *MA* surrounding XI (= eleven) – the team in question.

To *ANIMATE* is to ENLIVEN = NLI (= NIL, or
NOTHING, MUDDLED) in EVEN (= EVEN BET).

73   The four-legged in the hint is, of course, a cat, the two-
legged a man. Three legs are the symbol of the Isle of Man.
CHURCH, ORATOR, IONIZATION and PHYSIO-
GRAPHY.

74   199 in the hint is CIC, the letters 'round about' – OM –,
– YN –, etc.

78   SOMERSAULTING is an AEIOU-word.

79   ORTANIQUE is a cross between an orange and a tangerine. (ORange + TANgerine = unIQUE)

80   TONGA in the hints is an anagram of TANGO, and
BURMA of RUMBA.

82   (i) TO BE OR NOT TO BE, THAT IS THE QUES-
TION: THAT IS THE ANSWER.

(ii) AS DEAD AS DODOES.

89 STRIPTEASE; INTERROGATIVES; DECORATIONS; INSATIABLE; DISINTEGRATING; ANTAGONIST.

90 The line appears in *Julius Caesar*, by William Shakespeare.

91 MARCH (CHARM); APRIL (PILAR), MAY (YAM). Is it mere coincidence that these form an adjacent quarter of the calendar? Professor Didipotamus thinks that it is *highly* significant.

92 Let $0.1111\ldots = X$. Then $10X = 1.111\ldots$. So $9X = 1$ and $X = \frac{1}{9}$. Similar proofs hold for $0.\dot{a} = \frac{a}{9}$.

$\frac{1}{2} = 0.5 = 0.4\dot{9}$. When this puzzle was published in *The Guardian* an astonishing number of people wrote to say that $0.4\dot{9}$ was only approximately equal to 0.5. This is not so. $0.4\dot{9}$ is *exactly* equal to 0.5. $0.4\dot{9}$ must not be conceived of as having a finite number of 9s or having a last digit.

Let $0.49999\ldots = Y$ and $0.9999\ldots = Z$. Then $10Y = 4 + Z$.

$100Y = 49 + Z$. So $90Y = 45$ and $Y = \frac{1}{2}$, exactly, which is what we set out to prove.

93 fEAsT; VARIEgateD; asSUREd SpOIL; NoURiShED SKILLfulness; WHIMSies; APposiTe; RUINation.

97 ABCDE-FGHIJ is to be minimised. A must be more than F and BCDE should be as small as possible, GHIJ as large as possible. BCDE msut be 0123; GHIJ must be 9876. Hence 50123-49876 = 247.

98 NEWNESS (ES)

100 *SX*

118 Consider three numbers A, B, & C, each of which has an integral part and a fractional part. (For example with $33\frac{1}{4}$, 33 would be the integral part and $\frac{1}{4}$ the fractional part) and the fractional parts are a, b & c respectively. If we know that $A + B$, $B + C$ and $A + C$ are all whole numbers, then we can easily show that A, B, & C are integral or half-integral. If $A + B$ is a whole number the fractional parts add to a whole

216

number, so $a + b$ is a whole number. Similarly $b + c$ and $a + c$ are whole numbers. Adding all three: $a + b + a + c + b + c$, which equals $2a + 2(b + c)$ is a whole number. $2(b + c)$ is a whole number since $(b + c)$ is, so $2a$ must be a whole number, so a must be integral or half-integral. Similarly for b and c.

124 Let the sum of the digits occupying the hundreds places be H and the sum of those occupying the tens places be T. The equation can be written:
$100H + 10T + (45 - H - T) = 999$

This simplifies to: $99H + 9T + 45 = 999$. Dividing both sides by 9 gives: $11H + T = 106$.

At most every second digit in 1234567890 could be a tens digit and $1 + 3 + 5 + 7 + 9 = 25$, so $T = 25$ or less, so as $106 - T = 11H$, $11H$ must be 88 or 99, which leads to:
$H = 8$ & $T = 18$
$H = 9$ & $T = 7$.

If the hundreds digits sum to 8, they could be: 8; or 1 & 7; or 2 & 6. If the only hundreds digit is 8 we have 1234567 + 890 = 999 and so there is already a tens digit of 9 and since if $H = 8$, $T = 18$, we need a further digit sum of 9. $1 + 3 + 5$ and $3 + 6$ are the only possibilities, leading to:

$12 + 34 + 56 + 7 + 890 = 999$
$1 + 2 + 34 + 5 + 67 + 890 = 999$

These in fact turn out to be the only solutions.

126 (b) See also prime numbers, Appendix No. 7.

(f) BANQUETS.

128 Any series in which the numbers increase (or decrease) by the same amount as one goes from one term to the next is called an 'arithmetic series'. The difference between successive terms is called the common difference. It is easy using the method of the solution to find the Nth term of any such series. For example:

The series: 19, 28, 37, 46 . . .

The common difference is clearly 9. So we can write the series thus:

$(10 + 9), (10 + 2 \times 9), (10 + 3 \times 9), (10 + 4 \times 9) \ldots$

So the Nth term will be: $10 + 9N$.

129 We can write $711 \ldots 11116$ as $700 \ldots + 111 \ldots 100000 + 11116$. The sum of three numbers will be divisible by 7 if all three numbers are divisible by 7. Also if the sum of three numbers is divisible by 7 and two of the numbers are divisible by 7, the third must be divisible by 7 too. Now $7000 \ldots$ is divisible by 7 as is 11116. So we require $111 \ldots 100000$ to be divisible by 7. So we want $111 \ldots 1$ to be divisible by 7. The shortest such sequence is $111,111$.

135 Igor Belvoir knew that the bigger two numbers are, the bigger the number you get when you multiply them together; or, as Dr Yamamoto would say, the bigger two numbers, the bigger their product. To make a number as big as possible, you put all the large digits first. So in the calculation:

$$ABCDE$$
$$\times \: FGHIJ$$

make A & F be either 8 & 9, or 9 & 8; make B & G either 6 & 7, or 7 & 6, and so on. This makes the best use of the big digits. So:

A & F = 8 & 9, or 9 & 8; B & G = 6 & 7, or 7 & 6;
C & H = 4 & 5, or 5 & 4; D & I = 2 & 3, or 3 & 2;
E & J = 0 & 1, or 1 & 0.

This narrows things down a little, but we are still spoilt for choice: since for each digit pair listed there are two possibilities, there are $2 \times 2 \times 2 \times 2 \times 2 = 32$ possible pairs of numbers. How do we choose the one which gives the maximum product? First note that all 32 numbers which obey the restrictions listed all *sum* to the same number: 183,591. To see this, consider the sum:

$$ABCDE$$
$$+ FGHIJ$$

We know that $A + F = 17$; $B + G = 13$; $C + H = 9$; $D + I = 5$ and $E + J = 1$. So the sum will consist of 17 in the ten thousands column, 13 in the thousands column, 9 in the hundreds column, 5 in the tens column and 1 in the units column:

$$170,000 + 13,000 + 900 + 50 + 1 = 183,951.$$

Now, as it points out in the Hints, to split a number into two parts which multiply to a maximum, make the two parts as near to each other in size as possible.

In other words, out of the 32 pairings we were considering, each of which adds to 183,951, the pairing which gives the maximum product will be that where the two numbers are closest to each other in size. This will be achieved by making the number $9 - - - -$ have the smaller digits and $8 - - - -$ the larger digits. So the solution is: 96420×87531.

136 We are looking (so reasoned Lord Belvoir) for two whole numbers totalling 200, one of which is divisible by 17 without remainder and the other of which is divisible by 11 without remainder. He then subtracted multiples of 17 from 200 until he was left with a number divisible by 11 without remainder (i.e. a multiple of 11):

$200 - 17 = 183$ (no joy — not a multiple of 11.)
$183 - 17 = 166$ (no joy — not a multiple of 11.)
$166 - 17 = 149$ (no joy — not a multiple of 11.)

Belvoir was all set to give in, when:

$149 - 17 = 132$ (Bingo! — a multiple of 11.)

So four 17s and twelve 11s = 200. The number of men could have been 132 and the number of women 68. In which case, the long and short of this Iambic tale is that four women were sent down and 12 men. This is in fact the only possible solution.

139 Mr Yamamoto explains it thus:

The operation $(X,1)$ reduces by $S = X - 1$ all groups of commas containing X or more commas. Groups containing $X - 1$ (that is S) commas are unaffected by the operation. So after the operation groups of at least S commas still remain.

If the range is initially $1–N$, that is, if there were all numbers of commas from 1 to N to begin with, there will certainly be a group afterwards which contains $N - S$ commas.

The new maximum number of commas occurring, that is the new range, will be either S or $N - S$, depending which of the two is larger. The range will be least if $N - S = S$, that is when $S = \frac{1}{2} N$.*

The best we can do with each operation, then, is to halve the range. Initially the range is all numbers of commas 1–64; to reduce this to 1–32, we need a reduction of 32, which requires the operation to be (33,1). Similar arguments apply to the next steps.

* This is analagous to cutting an N-inch ruler into two pieces one measuring S inches and the other measuring $N - S$ inches in such a way that the length of the longer piece is as short as possible. This will be the case if both lengths are the same: i.e. $\frac{1}{2}N$.